# THE WHOLE WORLD
# SINGS

*The fans behind*

# *Barry*
# *Manilow*

*by*

# *Mandy Strunk*

# THE WHOLE WORLD
# SINGS

*The fans behind*

# Barry
# Manilow

*by*

# Mandy Strunk

DOWLING PRESS, INC.
NASHVILLE, TENNESSEE

Cover Design and
Interior Design by BookSetters
bksetters@aol.com

Back cover painting by
Shaquita

# Table of Contents

Introduction . . . . . . . . . . . . . . . . . . . . . . . . . . . . . . .7

Acknowledgements . . . . . . . . . . . . . . . . . . . . . . . . . . . .13

Dedication . . . . . . . . . . . . . . . . . . . . . . . . . . . . . . . . .15

Chapter One:     Basically Barry . . . . . . . . . . . . . . . . . . . .17

                 Just the Facts . . . . . . . . . . . . . . . . . . . . .17

                 Awards . . . . . . . . . . . . . . . . . . . . . . . . . .18

                 Credits . . . . . . . . . . . . . . . . . . . . . . . . . .18

                 Discography . . . . . . . . . . . . . . . . . . . . . . .19

Chapter Two:     Somewhere Down the Road:
                 The Pilgrimage to Manilow . . . . . . . . . . . . . .21

Chapter Three:   I Was a Fool: Barry Blunders . . . . . . . . . .69

Chapter Four:    Can't Smile Without You . . . . . . . . . . . .81

Chapter Five:     Read 'em and Weep . . . . . . . . . . . . . . .113

Chapter Six:      Even Now . . . . . . . . . . . . . . . . . . . . .131

Chapter Seven:   I'm Your Man, Barry Up Close and Personal . . . . .161

Chapter Eight:    Barry Manilow Fan Clubs . . . . . . . . . . . . . . .189

# Introduction

I can't remember a time when I didn't listen to the music of Barry Manilow. I grew up with his music and I always called myself a Barry Manilow fan. After all, I am a "Mandy." But, it wasn't this classic piece that I can thank for bringing me to his music. It was actually the *Barry Manilow Live* album itself that snagged me — hook, line and sinker. When my other friends were grooving to the Bay City Rollers and Shaun Cassidy, I was beginning a journey with a musician who engraved beautiful lyrics and clean, timeless rhythms into my soul.

I distinctly remember spending many nights alone in my bedroom in our rural home in Upstate New York, listening to the *Live* album, and singing along with Barry's smooth, infectious voice. I curled up in my bed with a flashlight in hand looking at the pictures on the album jacket over and over again. I fantasized about how glamorous Barry's life must have been playing music, traveling the globe, meeting exciting people and watching his dreams come true. I, too, had dreams of my own.

I was not able to attend any of Barry's concerts and I didn't know anybody else whom I could talk to about how his music spoke to me. I didn't know anything about him except for the morsels and tidbits pieced together in the latest issue of *16 Magazine* or *Tigerbeat* that I read religiously. Life went on, and I chose a career to pursue and wound up at a private college. I went from my tiny town to a tiny college nestled in a lot of trees of the Adirondack mountains.

I soon found that my musical taste was not exactly the "norm" for one's college heyday. My new dormmates played the Beatles, Black Sabbath, and the Stones. Being open-minded, I vowed to myself that I would take in the full college experience, including opening my ears to these sounds I never would have placed on my record player at home. Although I could appreciate the contribution these "new-to-me" artists made to music, I couldn't get myself much past Duran Duran. Needless to say, my *Barry Manilow Live* album came home with me on my next visit. I carefully stored it away in my bedroom thinking I was closing out a chapter in my life, for good.

A decade later, while living in a small town in Southern Indiana, the Barry Manilow CD section in my local Wal-Mart caught my eye. As I stopped to look at his material, I thought to myself, "Barry Manilow. It has been ages since I heard his voice." While thumbing through his material, I couldn't believe what I saw — *Singing With the Big Bands*. Barry Manilow recorded a CD singing Big Band tunes? How perfect. My all-time favorite artist does Big Band, another of my favorites. I scooped it up, hurried home and turned it on. There it was, that voice. Why hadn't I listened to his music in so long? It had been over 10 years. What was I thinking?

It wasn't until August, 1997, that the opportunity presented itself for me to see Barry live, in concert. And it wasn't until I began researching for this book that I found out I was certainly not Barry's most faithful fan. (That should go without saying provided my 10 year drought.) I was truly a babe in those Adirondack woods when it came to following his career. My education in fan loyalty was about to begin.

# A Book Is Born

The venue was Deer Creek Music Center in Noblesville, Indiana, located just outside of Indianapolis. My local radio station, WBIW in Bedford, was promoting Deer Creek's upcoming concerts, including

Barry's concert. After learning of the concert date, I decided not to let this opportunity pass me by. After all, I might not have another chance to see him in concert, or so I thought.

Deer Creek Music Center, an outdoor facility with pavilion seats, offers lawn seating as well. Hearing that I was a Manilow admirer, my friend and WBIW morning show personality, Jeff "JW" Williams, gave me two complementary concert tickets for the lawn. I was extremely grateful, but, he didn't understand that it was not enough for me to sit an acre from the stage. This is Barry Manilow of *Barry Manilow Live* for crying out loud! I had to be closer. Unfortunately for JW, but fortunately for me, his recent break up with a girlfriend left him with an extra ticket much closer to the stage. I stressed to JW how important it was for me to experience this long awaited moment from a closer vantage point, so, JW offered for me to go with him to the concert.

The concert date arrived but it still didn't sink in that I was going to see Barry Manilow perform live. We arrived at the venue, took our seats and prepared to enjoy the evening. Barry Manilow was on his "Tour of the World" promoting the *Summer of '78* release. I had purchased the CD a few weeks prior to the concert and actually cried the first time I heard it. I was around 12 years old when the original releases of these songs were wafting across the air waves. Many vivid memories of my adolescence rushed back as I heard Barry's voice.

After the opening act and a brief intermission it was time for Barry to hit the stage. Suddenly, I heard music, familiar music. It got louder, and louder. The lights began dancing their tribute to the legend who was only moments away from walking out to greet his frenzied audience. Then I saw a shadow move across the stage and the spotlights circled to land on one solitary man in the middle of the stage. I couldn't believe my eyes. It was Barry Manilow. He opened his mouth and that velvet voice filled the balmy air.

I ran the gamut of emotions that night as I sat and stood and sat and stood again, honoring the man, the voice, the songs. All I could think was how profound this moment was in my life. All of the songs that were my solace as a young girl became real to me that evening. As if I were in a time warp, my complete attention was focused on that man, that mesmerizing man. This was the artist I listened to in my tiny bedroom and with whose music I had dreamed those impossible dreams. This was the entertainer I had that radical connection with. Although it may sound strange, it was never a crazy teen-aged, love sick fantasy that drew me to Barry Manilow's music. I had a deeper association, and to this day, I still can't put my finger on it. Once in our lives, at best, we are able to identify with or are impacted by another person or their talent so completely that it eternally alters our lives. Even if you don't know them personally? I think so. I turned to JW, who by the way had his mouth wide open in awe, and I said, "Do you realize that we are witnessing an icon of our generation?" He agreed.

Barry's performance came to an end far before I wanted it to. Shaking myself out of an altered state that had washed over me during the concert, I purchased my Manilow T-shirt. Like cattle, we shuffled out of the venue to our cars. On the way home we could not stop talking about the concert. All I knew was that I had to see Barry perform again. The next day, I consulted my newly-purchased Manilow T-shirt and according to the concert schedule listed on the shirt, Barry was winding up his tour. The next "logical" place for me to see him perform was in Atlantic City, New Jersey. My college roommate, whom I had not seen since graduation, lived in Atlantic City, so, this would be an opportune time to visit her and catch the concert too. I phoned her in Atlantic City and began making arrangements for the trip. I'd given my extra lawn seat concert tickets to a friend, so I asked if she would like to fly with me to Atlantic City to see Barry in concert again. She was up for it. We organized a last minute yard sale to raise some funds for the excursion and a few days later, we were on our way to Atlantic City.

We arrived in Atlantic City the afternoon of the concert and after checking into our hotel room, we went to The Sands Resort & Casino, where Barry would perform, to pick up our concert tickets.

Because of general admission seating that evening, we arrived at The Sands' Copa Room approximately three hours prior to the concert to jockey for position for prime seating. While we waited in line, we began talking to those standing around us. Stories of devotion to Barry's career unfolded as people told how they traveled around their states, around the US, and around the world to go to Manilow concerts, CD signings, and TV appearances. I heard how people planned family vacations to include a

Manilow concert. I spoke to fans of 20 plus years as well as adolescent fans. Because this fan world was new to me, I began exchanging phone numbers and e-mail addresses so I could begin corresponding with these people. It became obvious to me that an instant bond occurs between people who enjoy Barry's music.

The day after the concert my "Barry Buddy" and I planned to go sightseeing since neither of us had ever been to Atlantic City. As we reminisced about the events of the previous evening, I had a profound revelation. "This has a book written all over it" I said to her. I was speaking about the fan phenomena. After returning home, I began researching books written by and about Barry Manilow and his fans. I discovered that the last book of this nature was his own autobiography, *Sweet Life: Adventures On The Way To Paradise,* published in 1987. There had not been a book written about his fans. The rest, as they say, is history.

While researching for this book, I have been privileged to work with hundreds of Barry Manilow fans. I have made many friends and associates because of this project. One of the most important things I have learned throughout this process is that Barry's fans are unique individuals who have fulfilling lives, wonderful families, and enriching careers. The common denominator among these folks is they, too, have experienced that "radical connection" with Barry Manilow and his music and they have chosen to enrich their lives by including his music and career in them. Some have shared touching and heartfelt stories with me for this book that they have never told anyone before. Some had me rolling on the floor with laughter because of the hilarious experiences they have had following Barry's career. We have laughed together, we have cried together, but most of all, we learned to care about each other.

Why put this book together? Simple. Not only do the fans of Barry Manilow warrant a book devoted solely to them, but, the stories you are about to read transcend the obvious subject of the book, the fan following of Barry Manilow. These stories are about human nature; our power to persevere no matter what the odds, our ability to laugh at ourselves and the world around us, and our capacity to love ourselves and each other.

No matter where we live, what we do for a living, what our religious persuasion might be, or what our ethnic background is, we are all very much alike. The fans of Barry Manilow are like a huge family, not void of their internal squabbles and achievements. They are a support system for each other using phones, e-mail, and snail mail. Their admiration for Barry has bonded many of them together in a unique way.

But perhaps the most profound lesson I learned throughout my journey researching and writing this book is that nothing mortal should suffocate the power we each possess within ourselves to accomplish whatever it is we are compelled to do. The principle here is simple. If you are passionate about something, do whatever it takes (legally and ethically, of course) to pursue it. The journey won't always be easy and it will not be without a little bit of blood, a fair amount of sweat, and a few tears. But, the satisfaction you receive will be priceless.

Did I have any great talent to write a book? Not really. Not being a writer by trade, I had to learn, from scratch, about the many intricacies of publishing protocol. I began by reading about the industry and asking many professionals a lot of questions. I asked a lot of questions. Above all, I put God in control of this book. I believe that God will use people and circumstances to perpetuate His purpose. As insignificant as some issues really are and as insurmountable as we often make them out to be, God has a plan and He will bless us when what we do perpetuates His plan.

This book is about the fans, for the fans and by the fans of Barry Manilow. Throughout the pages their many talents are showcased. Pay special attention to photo credits, drawings, and the stories themselves. The individuals who shared their talents for this book are very special to me. Thank you for seeing my vision, believing in this dream, and helping to make it a reality.

Oh, and that *Barry Manilow Live* album…. It has made many moves with me throughout the years and holds a place of honor in my personal memorabilia. But now, I listen to it on CD.

—*Mandy Strunk*

# *Acknowledgements*

*There are many people who were instrumental in this book's development and I want to thank them for their involvement, support and encouragement.*

To my Heavenly Father for His mercy, grace, and wisdom. Without Him I am Nothing. Matthew 6:33

S.W. Strunk. You know.

To my family for tolerating me through the highs and lows of research and writing. Thank you for listening, laughing, and loving.

To all of the fans who gave their encouragement, insight, time and contributions to this project, you are very special to me. Thank you for understanding my purpose for the book and unselfishly sharing your lives with me.

Special thanks go to the following friends and colleagues for their guidance, wisdom, and advice: Kyle S. Brant, Ron Dante, C.K. Lendt, Fred Vail, Jay Warner

Special acknowledgements go to the following for helping me with research, travel details, personal assistance, and for generally keeping me informed: Laura Conners, Tami Grafe, Carol Henning, Frank and Linda Horner, Gloria Jean Lewis, Barbara Lovejoy, Nancy Rosebrugh, Darlene Schwartz, Ann Underwood, Manimodems On-Line Barry Manilow Fan Club and to Jeff "JW" Williams for taking me to my first Barry Manilow concert.

# *Acknowledgements*

## ——*14*——

Thank you to Maryglenn McCombs of Dowling Press for sharing my vision, allowing me to take an active role in the book's progression, and for assisting me in making a dream come alive.

On behalf of fans around the world, I would like to thank Barry Manilow for the years of spectacular music, musicianship, and entertainment. You have given us music that we have danced with, related to, laughed and cried over, built relationships because of, and discovered ourselves through. It is impossible for you to know every fan by name, but do know that each one has a special story to tell about how your music has influenced our lives. We have been and will continue to be blessed by your life and songs.

To the support staff and colleagues of Barry Manilow, past and present, thank you for assisting him, enabling him to pursue his work and produce a quality and heartfelt product.

There are many others, too numerous to mention, who were constant sources of support, helpfulness, and exhortation. You know who you are and I thank you.

# *Dedication*

Dedicated to the fans of Barry Manilow

I t's your dream…Dream it as big as you want it.

—Helen Hazen, 1918-1997

# Chapter One

# Basically Barry

## Just the Facts!

Born:  Barry Alan Pincus
Date of birth:  June, 17, 1946
Raised:  Brooklyn, New York
Graduated:  Brooklyn Eastern District High School
Attended:  Julliard School

## Pre- "Mandy"

♪  Music director of play, *The Drunkard*.

♪  Music director for CBS-TV series, "Callback".

♪  Writer and arranger of numerous commercial jingles including: State Farm Insurance, McDonalds, Pepsi, Dr. Pepper, Band Aid, Kentucky Fried Chicken, and more.

♪  Music director, pianist and arranger for Bette Midler

# And then along came "Mandy"

1974, *"Mandy"* became Manilow's first #1 single!

## Awards and then some

- ♪ Recipient of Grammy, Tony, and Emmy Awards
- ♪ For albums produced for other artists including Dionne Warwick, Bette Midler and Nancy Wilson, he was nominated for Grammy Awards. Also produced albums for Lady Flash and Phyllis Hyman.
- ♪ Nominated for an Academy Award
- ♪ Received Oscar nomination for *Ready To Take A Chance Again* from film, *Foul Play*
- ♪ Plus: A string of Top 40 hits

## Author, Author

Autobiography, *Sweet Life: Adventures on the Way to Paradise*, 1987, McGraw-Hill

## Musicals

- ♪ *Barry Manilow's Copacabana*
- ♪ *Harmony*

## Film and Television

- ♪ Arranger and lyricist for "American Bandstand"
- ♪ Song, *Ready To Take A Chance Again*, for film, *Foul Play*
- ♪ Arranger, lyricist and vocals, *We Still Have Time*, for film, *Tribute*
- ♪ Character, Tony Starr in *Copacabana* (TV)

♪ Composed song for soundtrack of Walt Disney's *Oliver and Company*

♪ Composed for soundtracks, *The Pebble and the Penguin* and *Thumbelina*

## *30 and counting: Albums*

*Barry Manilow I*
*Barry Manilow II*
*Tryin' To Get The Feeling*
*This One's For You*
*Barry Manilow Live*
*Even Now*
*Barry Manilow Greatest Hits*
*One Voice*
*Barry*
*If I Should Love Again*
*Live In Britain*
*Oh, Julie!*
*Here Comes The Night*
*Barry Manilow Greatest Hits Volume II*
*Barry Manilow 2:00 AM Paradise Café*
*Manilow*
*The Manilow Collection Twenty Classic Hits*
*Barry Manilow In Copacabana*
*Swing Street*
*Barry Manilow*
*Barry Manilow Greatest Hits Volume I*
*Barry Manilow Greatest Hits Volume II*
*Barry Manilow Greatest Hits Volume III*
*Because It's Christmas*
*Barry Manilow Live On Broadway*
*Barry Manilow: The Complete Collection And Then Some*
*Barry Manilow Showstoppers*
*Barry Manilow Singin' With The Big Bands*
*Summer of '78*
*Manilow Sings Sinatra*

## Television Appearances

Too many to mention!! Ranging from his award winning specials to news programs and talk shows around the world. You name it, he's on it. And when the TV ratings need to be high, who do they call—Barry Manilow!

## Charity and Civic Activities

Manilow supports a variety of organizations and also contributes his time and talents performing various benefit concerts and making personal appearances for a multitude of charities and organizations including those which work closely with AIDS education and research.

Don't forget the thousands of concerts he has performed to sold-out crowds all over the world. *Rolling Stone Magazine* dubbed him *The Showman Of Our Generation.*

*Note, this index reflects Barry Manilow's career highlights and is not exhaustive.
Sources:  BMIFC, Arista, & Internet

# Chapter Two

# Somewhere Down The Road: The Pilgrimage to Manilow

You've heard the phrase, "Getting there is half the fun." For thousands of Barry Manilow fans, the quest to see Barry at concerts, signings and personal appearances has resulted in some exciting adventures. Wherever the destination, these fans always manage to have a little fun, make some new friends, and create memories that will last a lifetime.

Sometimes, there is no literal or physical destination. The pilgrimage may simply be a refreshed state of mind, creating a new way of thinking, or using Manilow music as the vehicle to overcome a circumstance or accomplish a task. Music is a powerful tool and Manilow fans use this power to achieve positive results.

Don't think for a minute that these folks take themselves too seriously, though. Humor is a healthy ingredient in this delicious recipe. As you will read, what these fans go through for Barry Manilow is sparked by an extreme and genuine respect for him and his music. The things that happen to them along the way just makes their journey's-end that much sweeter.

Just a portion of Jean's Barry Manilow Collection.

*Barry Manilow first entered* Jean Phillips's life when she was a teenager. Jean was 13 years old when she discovered the song "Mandy," and had to be content listening to Barry's music on the radio. Her allowance didn't allow her enough cash to purchase his records. But four years later, Jean got married — to another Barry fan. During the first few years of her marriage Jean, again, wasn't able to spend any extra money on Barry because of rent, groceries, utilities, etc.

In 1989 Jean and her husband moved to a larger house, which they have named "The Copa," and Jean devoted one entire room to her vast collection of Manilow memorabilia. Jean, well known around certain circles for her Manilow sundries, has a collection so extensive, she has become a celebrity of her own sorts, appearing on various television programs, and in a variety of newspapers and tabloids around England.

Jean's collection includes hundreds of items, many acquired from other countries including the United States, Japan, Germany, Australia, France, Spain, Russia, Thailand, and even Uruguay. Her Barry room is equipped with records, CDs, tapes, videos, posters, photos, and nearly every other Barry-related item she has been able to put her hands on. Jean has even stitched a Barry tablecloth for a table in the room and Barry curtains for the windows.

Jean attends as many Barry concerts as possible. In her quest, not even major surgery can stop her. When Barry performs in the UK, Jean makes every opportunity to see his performances. A few years ago, Jean had to have an operation, and she knew the timing of the surgery would fall between the date she bought concert tickets and the actual concerts. Under normal circumstances, the timing would have been sufficient. But, under abnormal circumstances, the timing was a disaster. Jean thought she would have the surgery, need a couple of days in bed to recuperate,

then she'd be ready to go to the concerts. But Jean's surgery wasn't that simple.

After 10 days in the hospital, the cherished moment of release arrived. She was told that her stitches would not be removed for another two weeks. She was to see Barry in concert in just four days. She asked her doctor if it would be all right for her to attend the concert. The doctor asked who was performing and Jean told him, "Barry Manilow." The doctor approved her attendance based upon his assumption that Jean would not be "exciting" herself at a Barry show.

Complete with 300 stitches, off to Cardiff Jean went with her husband and daughter. Ten days later, they went to another concert in Birmingham, this time, minus the stitches.

"Definitely the best medicine," laughed Jean.

To date, Jean has been interviewed over six times by newspapers wanting to know about her love for Barry and his music. She has also been a guest on several TV shows. According to Jean, one television appearance in particular stands out in her memory. This show had a debate format and it was live. The subject matter: people with obsessions. Guests on the show included a gentleman who collected glass bottles and a woman whose husband used to collect women's underwear (off other people's washing lines, no less). "And people think that I'm strange," Jean said.

Besides Jean, the other pro-Manilow representatives included a lady who had legally changed her last name to Manilow and a couple folks from a local Manilow fan club, Exeter Friends. Two other guests included a couple who divorced after allegedly, the husband read a newspaper cover to cover during a Barry concert and afterwards proclaimed, "Well, that was boring."

Opposing the Barry team was a panel of people in a variety of professions, including a music critic, a DJ, a musician, a psychologist and a number of non-Barry fans. One verbal battle ensued between the musician, Johnny Violent, and Jean. According to Jean, the Barry team emerged victorious with each rebuttal offered. "I don't know if they (the non-Barry representatives) thought that Barry fans were just a group of quiet, middle-aged women who were just going to sit there and take whatever was said, but, they were most definitely wrong," said Jean. Jean admitted that doing the show was great fun because the Barry fans were able to "have a go back" though the show's producer did ask them to refrain from hitting anyone.

"I've had a lot of great times over the years following Barry and I have some wonderful memories," Jean said. "But, Barry has also helped me through some very difficult periods, including the break-up of my marriage. The words in his songs are so true and the feeling and emotion he puts into them are straight from the heart. Thanks, Barry for everything."

*Hilary Stookes, the Newsletter* Editor for Barry Manilow's Exeter Friends Fan Club headquartered in Exeter, England, has been following Barry's career since 1982. Since then she has been invited to speak on the radio in support of Barry's *Copacabana*, and has also appeared on a local television program to talk about Barry and *Copacabana* before the show's opening in Plymouth.

Hilary had less than an hour's notice before her on-air appearance, but eagerly stepped up to the plate for Barry without much time to prepare or think about what she would say. Hilary didn't feel inconvenienced by the speedy summons. Instead, she was honored to have the opportunity to share her love for Barry.

Another distinct honor for Hilary was when she and members of her Exeter Barry Manilow Fan Club decorated Barry's dressing room when he appeared at Westpoint, England. Much care and planning went into the decoration process. The club had addressed all details, right down to the

Hilary Stookes, (far right), with fellow Exeter Barry Manilow Fan Club members.

identical red polo shirts printed with "Barry Manilow: Exeter 1993" for each of the club members decorating the room. The group made signs, posters and banners, blew up balloons, brought flowers and took loving care in decorating the room.

The group left several presents and cards on Barry's dressing table including Devonshire Cream Tea and a letter from the Mayor of Exeter welcoming Barry to the City. Their main present to Barry was a copy of *The Exeter Book*. Inside the book, Hilary and her group included a photograph of their club members donning their new red polo shirts. They each signed the photo and included the following inscription: "The Barry Manilow Appreciation Society (Exeter) has great pleasure in welcoming Barry Manilow to Exeter: 16 April 1993 - with affection and thanks for your beautiful music."

At the beginning of the concert, Hilary's group held up a "Welcome to Exeter" sign that was an exact copy of the one they left in Barry's dressing room. According to Hilary, when Barry recognized the club's signature red polo shirts and the banner he gave them a big wave.

"We knew then that it had all been worth it," said Hilary.

*For almost 20 years,* Barry Manilow's music has been a part of Sharon Lesage's life. Her first recollection of hearing his beautiful music was "Mandy" coming from the stereo in her sister's bedroom. That was in 1979.

At the age of 13, Sharon saw Barry in concert for the first time. Even at that tender, young age, she was absolutely struck by him. Sharon coerced her mother and aunt to take her and her cousin to Barry's concert in Lenox, Massachusetts. Long before she ever considered making a sign for the intensely-popular "Can't Smile" segment of Barry's concerts, Sharon and her cousin put the ingenuity of youth and innocence to work at making a sign of a different sort. Convincing her mom to use an old bed sheet, Sharon and her cousin got out the paint and went to work. They lovingly and carefully splashed, "We Love You Barry" on the sheet and gleefully hauled it with them to the concert. There, outside of the venue, they spotted a tour bus. Thinking that it was Barry's tour bus, Sharon and her cousin held the bed sheet in clear view of the tour bus for over an hour. But Barry was never seen on or near the bus.

Many years have passed since the making of that first sign, but the sign-making continues. In 1997, Sharon took her friend Michelle to her first Barry concert in Albany, New York. Michelle had been a fan of Barry's for many years but had never been able to attend one of his concerts.

What Michelle didn't know was that sly Sharon had a little surprise ready for a grand unveiling the night of the concert. When Sharon and Michelle arrived at the show, Sharon readied her sign and steadied herself for Michelle's reaction. The sign? "KISS MY GIRLFRIEND, PLEASE!"

*Lyn Arnold of Birmingham*, Alabama, and her Barry Buddy, Sherry, began making plans to attend two of Barry's 1997 concerts in Tampa, Florida, as they walked to their cars after his concert in Birmingham, Alabama, that summer. Lyn and Sherry, who both work and attend college, knew they would be on break from school and were looking forward to the concerts and getting away.

At 4:00 AM the day of Barry's first night in Tampa, Lyn and Sherry piled into the car. They had carefully planned this much-anticipated trip and knew they had ample time to drive to Tampa and make Barry's 8:00 PM performance.

No road trip to a Manilow concert would be complete without a vast array of Manilow tunes and Lyn and Sherry had that covered.

Just when they thought they were ahead of schedule, they came upon an unbelievable mess just outside of Gainesville, Florida, due to an accident and road construction. As they sat motionless watching the clock tick away, they started to panic. Not only did an hour pass by, but Lyn and Sherry had forgotten to factor in the time difference in Florida. They hadn't lost one hour; they had lost two. Lyn and Sherry panicked. Sherry got out of the car several times with the binoculars they brought for the concert to see if they could locate the trouble spot. What she saw was bumper to bumper traffic and a full-on, without-a-doubt catastrophe.

In desperation, Lyn and Sherry began plotting their escape from the endless line. Break through the road block that was guarding an exit onto the direction they were heading and go against the oncoming traffic? Sure. Shaking themselves out of their criminal stupor, they opted to obey the highway patrol officers. At one point, Sherry exited the car and ran about 20 cars ahead and pleaded with one officer, "Look, we are from Alabama and we have to get to Tampa by 8:00 PM to see Barry Manilow!" You can imagine how sympathetic the officer was to their plight.

With traffic at a standstill, they figured it was time to start bargaining with God for a way out of their troubles. (Currently, Lyn is supposed to give up her soap operas and start shopping at K-Mart. Sherry promised to take her pathophysiology class again for nursing school and enjoy it.) After losing approximately 2 1/2 hours, they arrived at their hotel around 7:00 PM, Tampa time.

Lyn stumbled into the hotel lobby and was more than ready to check in and take a long, hot shower, but, the desk clerk informed Lyn that she needed to phone home as her dog was very sick and it was an emergency. "At that point," stated Lyn, "I was absolutely sick to my stomach and shaking." She started to believe that it was just not meant for her to make this concert. She called home, with every intention of jumping back into the car and heading straight to her ailing dog. What she was told, somewhat to her relief, was that the vet wouldn't really know how the dog would be until the next day. So, Lyn decided she would wait until the next day to beat the path back home.

Where are all the good bellhops when you need one? Lyn and Sherry carried all of their luggage to their room by themselves leaving them with 45 minutes to make the 8:00 PM start. Mission accomplished. They showered, primped, and perfumed in record time and breathlessly crashed into their seats – fourth row seats.

Later during the show, Barry chatted with the person selected to use the clicker (a garage door opener-like device used to freeze-frame an on-stage screen of flashing album covers—Barry and band would perform a song from the album cover selected by pressing the clicker) and, according to Lyn,

Barry had asked if this person were from Tampa and then mentioned that sometimes people come from out of town to see the shows. Lyn and Sherry looked at each other and burst out in laughter. "If he only knew the trials and tribulations that some of us go through to see him," Lyn said. "Most people wouldn't go through all of that to see the Pope."

So, was all of this hassle worth it for Lyn? Absolutely. While she was at the Tampa concerts, she met several more Barry Buddies including a fan who had been traveling around by herself to see Barry's appearances for 12 years. When Lyn met her she told her, "I think I have been looking for you my whole life!" Chalk up another friendship made because of Barry. Even better still, when Lyn returned home, she found out that the ailing dog was just fine.

*Even though Jessica Watlington* is a young Barry Manilow fan, she has wanted to see him in concert since the first day she laid eyes on him. By most Manilow fan's standards, that wouldn't seem such a long time since most fans have followed his career longer than Jessica has been born.

Jessica's first exposure to Barry Manilow was in early 1997. She caught glimpses of Barry on the *A & E, Live By Request* promotions for Barry's upcoming performance, but, the real Manilow magic began on March 10, 1997, when Jessica saw "Summer of '78" on VH1.

At 19, Jessica is a full-time college student. But, when she is not hitting the books, she is absorbed in Barry's career.

Knowing Jessica's desire to see Barry in concert, her father orchestrated a little magic of his own. He purchased three tickets for Barry's Tallahassee, Florida, concert scheduled for December, 1997. For the big surprise, he placed the Ticket Master envelope containing the tickets in Jessica's CD tower close to her Barry Manilow *Greatest Hits* CD.

One evening, Jessica's father told her to get the CD, because he wanted to look at the song list. Jessica went to the CD tower and pulled out the CD, noticing a piece of paper sticking out of the tower. Thinking it was just an insert that came with one of the CDs, Jessica tried to shove it back in the tower. Jessica realized that this paper was not really supposed to be there and immediately felt nervous and jittery. Then, she noticed "Ticket Master" on the envelope. Jessica really started to shake, then. She opened the envelope and saw the tickets which read, "An Evening With Barry Manilow." She put her hand over her mouth and started to cry.

"Oh, no, you didn't," she yelled out. Jessica ran down 13 stairs, yelling and screaming "Thank You!" She raced into the kitchen and hugged her mother and father, thanking them over and over.

Jessica's mother was practically as surprised as she. Her mom didn't even know about the tickets until about five minutes before Jessica.

But, Jessica's story doesn't end here. Really, it is just the beginning of an unbelievable memory for Jessica. In preparation for the concert, Jessica and her dad made a sign for Jessica to take, in hopes that she might become the next "Can't Smile" girl. The night of the concert, the folks in line were told that they were unable to take their signs into the auditorium. Greatly disappointed but respecting this decision, Jessica threw away the sign she and her dad had put so much thought into.

When they reached their seats, they discovered that they were seated directly behind the sound boards. In desperation, Jessica, her mom, and dad, began talking to the ushers to see if there would be any possibility of moving to seats with a better view. The three were moved to the last row on the floor.

The concert began and Jessica was entranced. Jessica was so engrossed that she didn't notice when a lady approach her mother and began asking her if her daughter liked Barry. Her mom replied with a hearty, "She loves Barry." They were then told that there was one seat available on the front row and then asked if Jessica would like to be moved.

Jessica was given a ticket for her new seat and was instructed to walk toward the usher near the stage.

Jessica reached the usher and she showed her the ticket. As they were finding Jessica's seat, Barry began to move across the stage toward Jessica's side. Then, there he was. Jessica looked up and Barry was standing right in front of her belting out "Daybreak." Jessica broke out in a very healthy wave to Barry and enthusiastically yelled out, "Hi Barry" Jessica said that Barry gave a sweet smile, a head nod, a wink and a wave to her. The rest of the evening, Jessica's head was in the clouds.

So, why was Jessica selected from the hundreds of folks who could have been moved to that front row seat? Who knows! Jessica believes, though, that amongst the usher's chattering back and forth with each other, word got to the lady who ultimately approached Jessica's mom. Just a coincidence? Maybe – or, maybe not. Either way, Jessica has been branded a Manilow fan for life

*Do you remember when* Barry sang "It's Just Another New Year's Eve" on *Dick Clark's Rockin' New Year's Eve* special? Donna Desaulniers remembers it very well. She was at a friend's home celebrating the new year in the usual way. After they watched the ball drop, they left the TV on and continued with their party. Donna's attention was soon turned back to the TV when she heard this beautiful voice coming from the TV set.

"Something happened to me," explained Donna. "It was a very touching experience to me. At that time, with two small sons, I did not listen to much music on the radio. Believe it or not, I had never heard of Barry Manilow. I said to myself, 'Who is this terrific guy?'"

About a week passed and Donna was out doing some shopping. She went to her local record store, found the Barry Manilow section, and bought every Barry Manilow record in stock. This was only the beginning of her passion for Barry's music.

Even though she has listened to Barry's music for years, she did not attend any of his concerts until 1997. "I never had anyone to go with me," said Donna.

Donna and her husband decided to sell their house so they went to a local real estate agency for help. It was by no accident that Donna and her husband chose the agent they did. In conversation, Donna and her agent, Marge, discovered they both like Barry's music. Marge asked Donna if she had ever been to a concert and Donna told her that she had not, but, not because she didn't want to.

August 2, 1997, was the date that Donna and Marge began a new friendship. They went beyond real estate agent and client, they became "Barry Buddies." Barry performed at Foxwoods Resort & Casino and Donna and Marge were in the audience. Donna called for concert tickets and Marge's husband was their chauffeur. When Donna phoned a few weeks in advance for tickets, she was placed on hold. Expecting somebody to come right back on the line with prices and seat information, Donna patiently waited, and waited, and waited. Donna waited on hold for three hours. Finally, the ticket agent came back on the line and Donna secured two seats. "I was so happy that there were a few tickets left," said Donna.

Marge's husband dropped them off at Foxwoods a bit early so Donna and Marge hit the slots. Donna's mind was nowhere near the machines, though. "My mind kept saying, 'Barry is someplace in this building,'" Donna remembered. Time went by in slow motion for Donna. They got a bite to eat and then ventured to the concert hall and sat, waiting, waiting, and waiting some more for the show to begin. Finally, the music started and Donna's heart nearly skipped a beat. "There on stage, was Mr. Manilow in person," Donna said. "Tears came to my eyes. I had waited so long for this one moment of seeing him in person. I think I just sat and stared in the beginning and could not even remember what song he was singing. The whole show was terrific once I came out of my trance. It was an experience of a lifetime, one that will live in my mind and heart forever."

That night wasn't just another evening for Donna. It confirmed to her why she had listened to Barry's music all those years. "Down there on that stage was the person who has helped me through the years, changed my life for the better, and there I was in the same room as he was," said Donna. "I know that Barry will never know just how much he and his music has touched my life. It is with me daily and still helps me through the rough times."

Even though Donna and her husband have sold their home, they didn't move far and Donna hasn't lost contact with Marge. Donna and Marge shared a special moment together when they went to Barry's concert and they plan to share even more Manilow memories, somewhere down the road.

*"I was spending my vacation* at Puerto de la Cruz de Tenerife in 1975, was sad and lonely on a starry night while other people were dancing not so far from me. At once, I heard a song which sounded so different from the others; 'Mandy.' I knew that its singer was a certain Barry Manilow. I got the record and that was all," Guido Grassi recalled about his first exposure to Barry Manilow's music.

Guido's story continues: "In 1979, I was in Edinburgh and saw Barry in concert on TV. His smile, the way of meeting people, looked so special to my eyes and I said to myself, 'this kid really loves what he does and it shows.'" In 1980, Guido traveled from his home in Italy to the United States for the first time. During his visit, Guido purchased a few of Barry's albums and his true conversion began. According to Guido, this trip literally changed his life. Just two years later, Guido organized Italy's Barry Manilow Fan Club choosing UNICEF as his club's charity. It would be 10 years later that Guido's "Night of all Nights" came and changed his life one more time.

The date was May 12, 1990, and the place was Atlantic City, New Jersey. Guido remembers it well. It was the night Guido met Barry Manilow. "He is a wonderful man, so friendly and happy," Guido said. "To meet Barry was one of the strongest emotions in my life." While snapping a few photos, Guido's camera gave out. Guido said that Barry asked his assistant to bring in another camera. More photos were taken and later sent all the way to his home in Italy.

"I can relate to Barry in many things," commented Guido. "I'm full of enthusiasm like him, I'm a dreamer like him, I think he's strongly sincere, like I am too." Did Guido and Barry exchange any man-to-man advice during their brief encounter? "I gave him just one advice," remembered Guido, "to come to Italy and sing."

Guido, an author, has written an article, "A Beautiful Friend, Barry Manilow" which appeared in an Italian magazine. After a member of a Barry Manilow Fan Club in the states showed this article to Barry, he autographed a photo by writing, "Guido, Thank you for all your support. Ciao, Barry" and sent it on to him. Guido has also had seven books published in Italy. One of these books, *Cavalcata Americana*, includes that autographed photo of Barry. Incidentally, it was by showing this book to Barry's Assistant and Manager in Atlantic City that Guido was offered that opportunity to meet with Barry.

Even though his meeting with Barry was unforgettable, Guido has had something equally unforgettable happen because of Barry Manilow's influence in his life. Guido distinctly remembers the first time he fell in love. So, what does that have to do with Barry Manilow, you ask? In 1986, Guido met Giselle, who was president of the Brazil Barry Manilow Fan Club at the time, and fell head over heels for her. It was love at first sight and although their relationship lasted almost two years, fate had other plans. Now Guido is happily married to his love, Elena.

"Music is life and so Barry has changed my life," Guido stated. "His own music has been a true companion, a true friend, a true thing to dream of." To reach Guido or inquire about the Italy BMFC, e-mail him at ggrassi@hotmail.com.

*From the very beginning* I've always felt a special bond with Barry. Maybe it was that first song that got me interested and kept me that way. It's not so much a love affair, it's more of a friendship. A deep caring for someone you like," explained Betty Sadowski. Betty's friendship with Barry Manilow goes way back. It was the song, "All The Time" that became so meaningful to Betty almost 20 years ago when she was going through a rough spell in her life. It wasn't until 1980 that she got serious about Barry's music. "I guess that's when I came to realize just what it was I was hearing," Betty said. "I began to feel connected to Barry as a singer and joined the International Fan Club." Then, in 1982, she became involved in the newly established L.O.V.E. Barry Manilow Fan Club in Milwaukee, Wisconsin, of which she is president today.

Betty has what she calls a "club-load" of special friends that she travels with whenever Barry hits the road for his performances. But in particular,

Ann Underwood, also of Milwaukee, and Betty have developed a special relationship over the past few years. "I don't know if it's the similarity in age or experiences," Betty explained, "or if it's just that Manilow Magic." Whatever it is, Betty and Ann have had some pretty wild and memorable times together. On one of their adventures, Betty, Ann and the L.O.V.E. gang, literally lost their top.

On the return ride home from one road trip to see Barry in concert, the club crew created a convoy. With four in the first car, a mini-van, they didn't want to be cramped for space, so they secured their luggage in a car-top carrier. The carrier was attached to the top of the van with clamps hooked on the strips of metal that run along the top of either side of most mini-vans. Behind the van was a car carrying only two people. The driver of the second vehicle stayed close to the van throughout the trip.

A "club-load" of special friends, getting ready to see Barry.

The girls were almost home when, on the last leg of the trip, they began to pick up the pace. Being in the home stretch, they had plenty to talk about and time rolled by quickly as they recounted the events of the previous three days. Suddenly, Betty, who was driving the van, heard a strange, dull sound and really couldn't figure out exactly where the noise was coming from. It all happened so suddenly. She looked in her rear-view mirror to see if she had run over something in the road. It was the car-top carrier, bouncing merrily down the middle of the road. With the speed of the vehicle and the gusty winds that day, the car-top carrier had become airborne and launched off the roof, narrowly missing the car with their buddies right behind them.

As soon as she could, Betty pulled the van into the emergency lane and the second car did the same. They got out of their cars and ran across the two lane highway to find the carrier completely intact. They shoved the carrier into the car and made their way to the first exit ramp and off the expressway. They reattached the carrier to the top of the van, but this time, they opted not to put anything in it in case the carrier took a notion to take flight again. The luggage of four women was strategically loaded into the van and car.

When the gals recounted the experience, they were amazed that nobody was hurt. At the exact time that the carrier made its exit from the van, the car was not following anywhere near as close as throughout the rest of the trip, allowing them reaction time to swerve and miss running into the carrier. Had the car been at its usual distance, the carrier would have landed right on the hood of the car. To make matters worse, they were traveling through some major traffic and it was also a miracle that the carrier didn't cause an accident. "After our hearts started beating again, we suddenly realized that God had been watching out for us that day," Betty remembered.

"*I grew up in Iowa* and there just weren't many major concerts close enough to travel to," said Beth Chase. But after moving near Austin,

Texas, Beth now attends the occasional concert when acts come to town. But, the one performer Beth has always wanted to see since the "Mandy" days is Barry Manilow. Beth's first Manilow concert came in November, 1997.

"When I heard about the concert in Austin, I got tickets as soon as I could and then called my daughter to tell her the news," Beth said. Beth was so excited to finally be able to see one of her favorite singers perform live. Beth's 23 year old, alternative and hard rock music-loving daughter, Heather, wasn't as thrilled.

"We are going to a Barry Manilow concert," Beth told Heather. Heather's reaction was indifferent, at best. She even hinted that her mom might want to take someone else with her who might enjoy it more. "My daughter," Beth said, "is my best friend and I couldn't imagine going with anyone but her." Heather agreed to go, but Beth got the distinct impression that it was only to keep her company.

As the concert date approached, Heather was no more excited about going. That evening, as Beth and Heather were leaving the house for the concert, Beth searched for the binoculars she wanted to take to the show. She turned around to find Heather rolling her eyes at her.

When Barry first came out on stage, Heather chuckled. She couldn't believe she was at a Barry Manilow concert with her mother. By about the fifth song, Heather began to change her tune. Later in the evening, Beth looked over at her daughter and witnessed a huge grin on her face from ear to ear. She leaned over to her daughter and asked "Are you smitten with Barry?" After a long pause, Heather admitted, "Yeah, but don't tell anyone."

Emotions ran high after the concert in Austin. "We were 100% Barry Manilow groupies and did not want to see the show end. As we were leaving the Frank Erwin Center, we saw some women hanging over a cement wall, looking down at a huge tour bus. We were curious and so we started looking over the wall too. We were convinced that Barry was going to walk out of the building and get into the bus. We stood there in the cold for probably 30 or 45 minutes, but, no Barry. The security people said that Barry had left a long time before that. We stuck around a little longer, laughing at ourselves and talking to the other fans," Beth explained.

"He really knows how to work a crowd," Beth said. "He made us laugh, cry and we both left there being Barry Believers! I know that most men do not understand the attraction that women have for Barry Manilow, but there is definitely some magic there. I don't know what he looked like as a young boy, but, he is a very beautiful man today, inside and out. Being 'beautiful' isn't only how you look physically (although I think he is gorgeous) but, it's also how you present yourself, and you have to be yourself and earn the love and respect that you deserve—which Barry Manilow has done so well. The charisma that Barry has is unbelievable. It's magnetic, it's hard to take your eyes off him for even a moment when he's on stage. I think Barry should be an inspiration to everyone."

The destination: Rockford, IL

The motive: Barry Manilow concert

The crime: The car

Each year, it seems as if the auto makers produce vehicles even more sophisticated than the previous year's models. Some have automatic climate control while others boast navigational systems. Annette "Nette" Josleyn isn't so sure that her car doesn't think for itself.

Nette, her twin sister, Toni, and a bunch of their friends piled into Nette's one year old Bonneville SSE on route to Rockford, Illinois, from Merrillville, Indiana, for their most sacred ritual – to see Barry Manilow in concert. Before they left their hometown, they stopped at a gas station to fuel up. Nette topped the tank off, paid the attendant, and got back in the car, ready to get on the road. Nette turned the key and nothing happened. Nette tried again. The car was dead. How can this be? It was just running a minute ago. The car just would not start. On to Plan B.

One year later, the women had set out for the exact same trip. This "rite of passage" began in much the same way as the previous year. Everybody filed into Nette's Bonneville again. Lightning doesn't strike in the same place twice, right? Perhaps not, but, the Bonneville sure struck twice. Nette turned the key and the "Service Engine" light came on. Not again! Not wanting to repeat the previous year's fiasco, they opted not to take the blasted Bonneville and, instead, they took another car.

Nette decided that her car was not "Manilow friendly" and because of that, she demoted it. Nette's can't-be-relied-upon-to-get-to-a-Manilow-concert Bonneville was not allowed to make Manilow-related trips anymore. Instead, she used it to get to and from work. She replaced it with a new family car just one day prior to her becoming a "Can't Smile" girl at the Deer Creek Music Center near Indianapolis, Indiana. Sounds like a pretty good trade, don't you think?

*Debbie Cohen's appreciation for* Barry's music began while attending a college dorm party. (And you thought college kids only listened to The Doors and The Beatles!) She was around 18 years old at the time and "Mandy" made the song list that fateful evening. "I was happy that they finally played a slow song because I wanted to dance with this guy for a long time," said Debbie. So, it was really the guy she was interested in. The guy is not in Debbie's life anymore, but, Barry's music is.

Several years later, Debbie, now happily married with three wonderful children, incorporates her love for Barry in her life whenever she has the opportunity. During the summer of 1997, while attending one of Barry's concerts, Debbie heard an announcement advertising Barry's New Year's Eve concert at Universal Amphitheater in Los Angeles, California. She was thrilled as she and her family had planned their Christmas vacation in Los Angeles and they would be there for the majority of Barry's performances. Talk about great timing!

Debbie dashed home from the concert and began making arrangements to attend Barry's December 28th performance also scheduled at Universal Amphitheater. Fortunately, Debbie's mom was going with them, so, the baby sitting was taken care of. Debbie called the BMIFC (Barry Manilow International Fan Club) in California and inquired about concert tickets. The tickets were going to cost her about $30.00 more than the ones she purchased for Barry's show in her hometown, Pittsburgh. "I was going to see Barry again, who cared what they cost," Debbie said.

Debbie didn't exactly have the tickets as they weren't physically in her hot little hands. The BMIFC would send the tickets to her home and assured her that they would arrive before Barry's late December concerts. They were right. They did arrive at her home in Pittsburgh, but, Debbie and her family were already in California.

Debbie practically made her family crazy as she anticipated the arrival of her concert tickets. The time had arrived for their departure to California and she still had not received the concert tickets. (Keep in mind that Debbie's family vacation began during the week of Christmas.) She was in a quandary and didn't know what to do about the tickets. After much consideration, she decided to ask a neighbor to be on the lookout for a package from Starglow (where you can find a myriad of Manilow merchandise) or the BMIFC as the delivery would require a signature. Debbie even plastered her door and front porch with signs informing the unsuspecting mail carrier to deliver this prized package to her neighbor.

As promised, the package arrived at her home, on Christmas Eve day to be exact. Her neighbor braved the long lines at the post office to overnight the tickets to Debbie in California. But, something happened in transit and Debbie's tickets were nowhere to be found that next day. Debbie frantically phoned her neighbor to get the tracking number and then she called the post office. She stayed on hold with the post office for 45 minutes trying to locate the package

The post office came through for Debbie. Debbie was finally, definitely going to see Barry in concert on December 28th – maybe. Debbie and her husband were looking forward to the concert. They needed a break from their family vacation and an evening of romance was just what the doctor ordered. The doctor should have ordered medicine for a migraine headache too. The day of the concert, Debbie's husband was knocked out of commission with an excruciating migraine.

Driving down Santa Monica Boulevard, Debbie's hubby's sore stomach got the best of him. Her 13 year old daughter, Jamie immediately got worried, not about her father, but worried that her mother was going to make her go to the concert that evening. Her fears were well anticipated as Debbie turned to Jamie and said, "Guess who's going with me now?"

Without a choice, Jamie conceded to going to the concert making her mother promise that she wouldn't tell her friends that she went with her mom.

The evening of December 28th arrived and found Debbie and Jamie standing in line at the Universal Amphitheater. An announcement informing the concert-goers that no cameras would be permitted inside the venue, was made, and Debbie and Jamie had to think fast on their feet. After a day of sight-seeing, Debbie still had her camera in her purse. Not wanting to trek back outside to the parking lot and fight the long line again, Debbie and Jamie cleverly fashioned a false bottom inside her purse, concealing the camera. The camera was not detected as they made their way into the concert.

After everything Debbie went through to get to the concert, was she still able to relax and enjoy herself? Absolutely, even though the "seats weren't that great" said Debbie. That didn't matter, though. She was there with her daughter and in the presence of Barry Manilow. Debbie was not disappointed.

Jamie, however, got embarrassed when Debbie purchased a Manilow T-shirt and hat at the concert. Jamie informed Debbie that she couldn't wear them when she was with her. "I showed her," Debbie said. "I told her friends she was my date at Barry's concert."

*Dorie Woytovech now lives* in Texas, but, in 1978, while living in Miami, Florida, she attended a Barry concert at the Hollywood Sportatorium in Hollywood, Florida, that, to this day, she has not forgotten, and probably never will forget. The Sportatorium, according to Dorie, was nestled "way out in the boonies," and the route to the Hollywood Sportatorium had two lanes; one going to it and one leaving it. In what seemed to Dorie to have been a five mile backup, her car decided to provide the pre-show entertainment. As the traffic crawled, clawed, and inched its way to the Sportatorium, Dorie's car began to overheat. "I knew that if I broke down, the people who were in back of me would have pushed my car into the canal which was on both sides of the road," said Dorie. "So, I backed off a little from the car that was ahead of me so my engine could get some air and I made it."

Dorie's seat for the concert was located in the far reaches of the arena, but, Barry's white piano was in perfect view. "Barry looked pretty small, but during the second half of the show, he came out all dressed in black, leather, I think, with these big, dark sunglasses on. He looked real cool," Dorie explained.

Thankfully, her car performed just fine on the way home. Dorie recalls sitting in the line of traffic and watching a helicopter fly overhead from the venue. Dorie just knew Barry was aboard. She waved and said "Bye, bye, Barry, see you later." As promised, she has and will continue to see him for many years to come.

*Besides the fact that* Linda Phillips once confused Barry Manilow with Neil Sedaka, throughout the years, she become a big fan of Barry's. The first concert Linda attended was in 1976 when a fellow college student suggested going to see Barry perform at the Mississippi River Festival in Illinois. Even though the festival does not take place anymore, at the time, it was a big deal. Linda agreed to go even though she had no idea who Barry Manilow was. "The minute he walked on stage, I was thunderstruck," Linda recalled. "He was awkward, he was lanky, and yet, I could tell that there was a raw talent. I knew it from that moment that he was good." At the time, Barry had three albums out on the shelves. Linda left the concert and immediately bought them all.

While attending a concert in Champaign, Illinois, in 1983, she was astonished to discover that there was actually going to be a convention for Barry Manilow fans later that year. Linda and her Mississippi River Festival pal planned to attend. Linda called the BMIFC (Barry Manilow International Fan Club) to make reservations for the convention believing that there were probably only going to be a handful of people at the event. Really, how many Barry Manilow fans were there, they thought. Well, the joke was on them when a few weeks later, Linda received a letter from the BMIFC informing them that the hotel where the convention was to be held had been completely booked up and they would have to choose an alternate place to stay. "We knew we were on to something," Linda said.

By 1984, Linda had already co-founded her Barry Manilow fan club, Manilow Music of Missouri. That same year, Linda had written the BMIFC asking permission to decorate Barry's dressing room at the St. Louis arena where he would be performing. Four days prior to the St. Louis concert, Linda had not yet heard from the BMIFC. Her fan club pals had tickets for Barry's performance in Kansas City scheduled for that fourth day before St. Louis. The days were ticking by and the club knew that they'd only have three days to prepare for decoration duty after they returned home from Kansas City.

The day of the Kansas City concert, the phone rang at Linda's home. Linda's mom answered the call. A gentleman asked if Linda Phillips was available. Linda's mom said, "Oh, no. She just left with three carloads of screaming girls for Kansas City." The caller asked if they were by chance headed to Kansas City for a show. "Yes," Linda's mom replied, "It's Barry Manilow, who are you?" The caller identified himself as Marc Hulett with Barry Manilow and proceeded to inform Linda's mom that Manilow Music of Missouri Barry Manilow Fan Club had received permission to decorate Barry's dressing room at the St. Louis arena.

Undaunted, Linda's mom continued the conversation. "You know," she went on, "I just have to tell you. When she first started liking this Barry Manilow, I just didn't even know what to think. She has got friends from all over the place. She has friends from Utah, New York,

Kansas City, England, and Japan. It is just amazing the friendship that is there."

Back in St. Louis, the half-way point of Barry's concert arrived and intermission was upon them. People parted ways to visit the restroom, stretch their legs, catch up with old friends, etc. Linda's friend Harriet approached her and said, "You are not going to believe who I just talked to." Linda was game. "Marc Hulett," said Harriet. Harriet escorted Linda to where Marc was standing and introduced them. According to Linda, Marc explained how he had called her home and spoke with her mother. Linda was in fear of what her mother told Marc. She was afraid that her mom, done only as a mother can do, told Marc her entire life history about her love for Barry Manilow, which was, in fact, true. Evidently, Linda's mother shared a lot with Marc. They were, after all, on the phone for over thirty minutes.

"*I have found that* the friendships Barry inspires among his fans are all very special and they do feel like family. Some are like 'distant cousins' who you see only at concerts, conventions, etc. But others reach deep into your soul and bind you like sisters and you know that they will be there for a lifetime. We call that 'Manilove,'" said Suzanne Swiss.

Over the 20 plus years Suzanne has followed Barry Manilow's career, she has made some fantastic friends. But, Suzanne has made one very special friend in Gloria Lewis. Several years ago, Suzanne and Gloria met at a fan club party for the Maryland Manilow Maniacs' BMFC. Their attendance at this fan club gathering was the first for both Suzanne and Gloria. After the festivities ended, Gloria gave Suzanne a ride home and during that ride, they shared their hearts with each other and an inseparable bond was formed.

Throughout the years Suzanne and Gloria have been through a lot together, Manilow-related and otherwise. In 1990 Suzanne was facing some serious surgery. That December, Barry was making an appearance in New York City to greet his fans and sign copies of his recent release,

*Because It's Christmas.* Suzanne was in no shape to attend this signing although every ounce of her being wanted so desperately to be next to Barry. Knowing her desire, Gloria quietly crafted a plan.

In the wee hours of that cold December morning, Gloria boarded a train into the city. She was on a mission for her Barry Buddy. After arriving in the city, Gloria, stood for hours outside the Tower Uptown building where Barry would be appearing. She was there so long, some people who were preparing for Barry's arrival, amazed with her dedication, gave her one of the 8 X 10 posters that had been used for publicity. Gloria had brought her own personal item to be signed by Barry too.

While in line waiting to meet Barry, Gloria heard that, in order to keep the line moving at a reasonable pace, Barry would only be signing one item per person. What would Gloria do? She really wanted to get Barry's signature for Suzanne, too. Gloria had to make a decision and after thinking about it, she decided it was more important to get Barry's signature for Suzanne.

When Gloria got to the table where Barry was seated, they greeted each other and began making small talk. Gloria began to talk about her best friend, Suzanne, who would be having surgery very soon and she told Barry that she was having him sign the 8 X 10 poster for her. Apparently touched by Gloria's unselfish gesture for her friend, Barry not only signed the poster for Suzanne, he autographed Gloria's CD as well.

Gloria presented the astonished Suzanne with her get well gift and

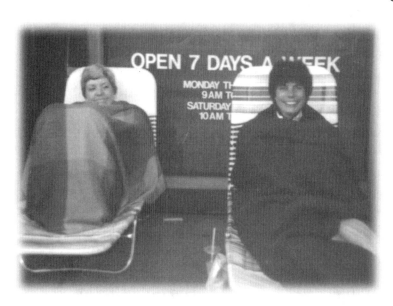

Gloria (left) and Suzanne, camping out to be the first in line at a book signing.
(Photo by Betty Gillman)

Suzanne was elated, so elated, she kept the picture with her throughout her hospital stay. The hospital staff got a charge out of Suzanne's special get well wish and one by one, they stopped in to check on "the lady with the Barry Manilow picture."

Suzanne's picture reads:
"Suzanne,
Get well soon,
Love,
Barry Manilow"

"Best medicine I ever had," exclaimed Suzanne.

Gloria, at an "In the Key of B" Fan Club gathering.

# Paradise Trail

## by Judy Kohnen

*It seems like years* since I took that trip across the Atlantic Ocean in January, 1998. However, the zeal of it, the adventure, the fun, the heart-moving experiences — all those things that stir the heart — they whir inside me, even now.

From America to the UK, I did venture. And alone, did I dare. I'd never traveled outside of the U.S.A. in my life, so it was definitely a challenge on my part, but one I don't regret taking, for the impressions it left on my life and the friends it acquired me are blessings I'll forever be thankful for.

What first turned out to be an unlikely, but fun-to-imagine trip to visit my e-mail friend Suze (better known to me as Royal Sis Suze) became "the real thing."

But back to the imaginable trip I'd take — it would, of course, be during the time when the talented singer/musician Barry Manilow would be touring England. How convenient! How fun and exciting! I've always thought when you dream, dream big. Being an aspiring writer, imagination has no bounds. Best-selling author/novelist, that's me — still in the dream stage, but hey, I believe in dreams. I know they come true. Barry knows they do, too. That's why he keeps reminding us to believe in ourselves and go for what we want in our lives.

I wanted to go to England in January to meet my e-mail Royal Sis, and see Barry again, this time in style. We're talking about something more high class than a limousine. We're talking "Maniloonie Fun Bus." All I had to do was search for yonder miracle, the one that would endow me with gobs of money to buy a plane ticket, a Fun Bus ticket, and several concert tickets. I forgot about hotel expenses and food expenses. But who could think about sleeping and eating at a time like this? Do you eat and sleep in your dreams?

One fine day, my birthday in fact, my miracle came. Funny thing, but my search for a miracle was on short hold that night for I was celebrating turning 40, with my family. But lo and behold, in a birthday card from my husband, was $500 with a note that read, "take a trip to England to see your e-mail friend." It was secret money he'd saved up for a family trip, that due to certain circumstances, we'd not be able to take during the time we had planned. So, he gave the money to me. So wonderful when people you live with love you. I had two months to raise the remainder of the money I'd need for lodging, concert tickets and eats. I'm a firm believer in "where there's a will, there's a way."

But enough of the drawn-out story. I went to England, I met my e-mail Royal Sis Suze, I met loads of British Barry fans, made lots of endearing friendships along the Paradise Trail in that stylish Fun Bus, even met my e-mail friend Jetty from Holland, and I saw Barry nine times in concert! Oh, but wait! I actually saw Barry 10 times, for during my first night in England, I sat center front row at the Jack Docherty Show!

I thought dreaming was BIG stuff, but my real life experiences turned out to be much bigger than my dream ever was. All the quick planning prior to my two week stay in England did not prepare me for the adventures forthcoming, and the near-celebrity experience I encountered. On TV, in the newspapers from the very start of the tour—our small and innocent Maniloonie group was hounded by reporters and photographers as we traveled the country on that Fun Bus. We all soon learned that the best thing to say was "no comment!" for no matter what you said, your words were guaranteed to be twisted when it went to press. So all of you out there who read those many articles plastered on the pages of national and local newspapers, don't even believe half of it. Cross out all the negatives and highlight the positives, for only the positives were the real truth and way of things.

One might think I took this trip because I was an idolizing Barry fan. No, no, no. I took this trip because I saw it as an adventure, an ultimate experience I was surely never to forget. I took it as a chance to learn more about the world and a culture I knew nothing about. I saw it as an exciting challenge to venture the world alone, to see if I could do it, see if I had the courage to do it, to meet people I've never met before. I took the trip to gain wisdom and friends. I accomplished them all.

I don't idolize Barry; I love him. There's a difference. Barry is definitely a man. Human. Not a god, though blessed by God. A man who possesses a passionate soul. He has feelings just like we do. He hurts like we hurt. It's important we keep our perspective and respect him for who he is. A man. He tries to help us in so many ways. I truly think that he's not here on this earth for fame, but as a helper and a teacher. We're not his disciples, but his students. Barry's blessed, we're blessed.

I'll never forget my UK trip and the wealth of knowledge and joy I derived from it. Birmingham. Bournemouth. Cardiff, Wales. London. My love and memories dwell in those cities and with those wonderful friends I met during my stay there. I love you all. I miss you all.

*In case you haven't* noticed lately, Barry Manilow's choice of clothing is impeccable, to say the least. Maybe you are in awe when you see him in one stunning ensemble after another, tour after tour. Perhaps you've wondered where he gets his fabulous clothing.

On June 17, 1989, Gloria Jean Lewis of Owings Mills, Maryland, and Suzanne Swiss of Baltimore, Maryland, had the unique opportunity to sit down with Phillip Dennis, Wardrobe Supervisor for Barry Manilow, and ask him a few questions. The following is an excerpt from that interview which took place at the Las Vegas Hilton Hotel and Casino.

## Behind The Scenes
*by: Gloria Jean Lewis and Suzanne Swiss*

GLORIA: **Could you give us some early background information on yourself, such as where you were born, your education, etc.?**

PHILLIP: *I was born in Salisbury, Maryland and was raised there up until I went to college. I went to art school in Columbus, Ohio, and got my Advertising Design degree in costumes. I graduated from college in 1979 and then I moved to Los Angeles, California, and started working out there.*

SUZANNE: **How did you become involved in this profession?**

PHILLIP: *In costumes? I knew at a very early age that I wanted to do costumes. Mostly, I remember watching television and seeing the Carol Burnett Show and the Sonny and Cher Show. I thought, 'Who is this Bob Mackie guy? He must have it made to be able to do this and make money out of it.' So, I was really interested very young and I knew very early what I wanted to do. The counselors in High School would always say, "Don't worry, you'll change your mind a thousand times while you are growing up," but I never did. So, I have always wanted to do it and I am very lucky.*

GLORIA: **Who else have you worked for before Barry?**

PHILLIP: *Well, the latest projects I did right before Barry were a couple of films for Michael Jackson. I did a film called "Captain EO" as the key costumer and a film with him called "Moonwalker." We did a big video in that called "Smooth Criminal."*

SUZANNE: **When did you join the Manilow entourage?**

PHILLIP: *I started in January of 1988.*

SUZANNE: **Did you know any of the group before joining up with Barry?**

PHILLIP: *No, none of them. I was recommended by a wardrobe friend in LA and so they gave me a call.*

GLORIA: **When a tour is being put together, what are your responsibilities?**

PHILLIP: *I sit down with the director and find out how many changes there are going to be, how much we are going to need, how many skits are going to be in the show. Actually, once we know what the look is going to be, I'm responsible for getting the costumes built, all the accessories shopped, and buying the supplies I'll need on the road. Also, I usually buy most of the hand props.*

SUZANNE: **What are your responsibilities after a tour is on the road?**

PHILLIP: *Basically, I set up all the dressing room areas. I decide who will go in which room, who needs the most space and where we need makeup mirrors, tables, lights. Then, I set up all the rooms, all the actors' costumes and I make sure they are all cleaned, pressed and repaired. If we need to replace something, I go out and shop - like shoes and hose. I set up all their makeup and all their hair supplies. Then during the show, I help with the changes.*

GLORIA: **How do you like dealing with the fans who are decorating the dressing rooms when you arrive? Did you have that type of thing to deal with when you worked for other people?**

PHILLIP: *I do admit, especially when we are doing one-nighters, it can be a little bit crazy. The fans are wonderful and very generous. On the whole, especially here and in Europe, they are all very sweet. It was interesting, when I was with Michael, the fans never got a chance to even get anywhere near a dressing room. I was a little surprised when I came on but after I thought about it I realized how much it means to you guys and he allows you into his rooms. I'm sure it makes you feel a little closer to him. You can visualize in your head what it's like back here.*

GLORIA: **Tell us about the costumes and how they come about?**

PHILLIP:   *They can come about it different ways. A lot of times, Barry will have a basic idea of how he wants to look. You have to think about whether it's a Summer or a Winter tour, do you want lightweight clothing or heavier things. Usually when we decide what Barry is going to do we will sort of build the others to go with it.*

GLORIA:   **What are they made out of and what do they cost?**

PHILLIP:   *It depends. It's real important when you construct them to realize that they are going to be on the road for a long time. They are going to be used over and over again. So, it's important to pick out fabric that one, won't be too hot and two, won't get wrinkled. How much they cost, no comment, but to get a good costume that will hold up, you have to spend money.*

SUZANNE:   **Does each person have a say in the design of their costume?**

PHILLIP:   *Yes. The band will wear anything, almost. The ladies each have their quirks. They each like different styles and fabrics so I listen to them and give them a say in their costumes.*

SUZANNE:   **Does Barry take part in the designing/buying of his clothes? In what way?**

PHILLIP:   *Absolutely. When he decides what he'd like to go for, he usually looks at sketches first and he'll approve those and we'll get some fabric swatches and he'll approve those. He's definitely interested in it all the way through.*

GLORIA:   **Who decides each night what outfit Barry will wear?**

PHILLIP:   *Usually on one-nighters, I'll put an outfit in the room and he'll wear it. Sometimes he will tell me what he wants to wear and other nights he'll put on whatever I have in there.*

GLORIA: **What is an average day on tour like in the life of Phillip Dennis?**

PHILLIP: *It depends on where we are. Usually, by 2:00 p.m. I try to be out of bed (big smile). If we're in a place for more than a day, I usually don't have to go in too early. If we're all set up, I go in an hour or so before Barry comes in and just set up his room—put that night's clothing in, rearrange, make some hot water for tea.*

SUZANNE: **What goes on after a show is over?**

PHILLIP: *There are usually a few guests that come backstage to meet Barry and talk for a little while. Barry is not one to hang out too late after a show. He likes to either get out and go have something to eat or go rest.*

*Following the career of* a superstar like Barry Manilow is nothing new for Monica Jeffress and her identical twin sister, Ann Browning of Bournemouth, England. You might say that Monica and Ann cut their teeth on a couple of other well-known groups from England. "We were naughty kids," Monica explained, "and we didn't go to school on days when a pop group was in town." Monica and Ann weren't happy to simply see these groups perform. Instead, they preferred the "royal treatment," rubbing shoulders with the band members and becoming their groupies.

In those days, it was easier to get close to a performer than it would be today. They would find out what hotel they were staying at, befriend the managers at the theaters or restaurants, and presto, they were in the presence of the band. "We got very friendly with Little Richard," Monica remembered. "He paid our fares and accommodations to tour around the North of England. This is how we got friendly with The Stones. The Beatles were friendly guys and remembered us from the word 'Go.' To this day, we can often see George and Ringo around the UK and we get a few friendly words."

But no other entertainer has touched Monica and Ann's lives like Barry Manilow. "Barry has helped Ann and me over serious illnesses over the years," said Monica. Not too many years ago, Monica and Ann were both told they had life-threatening medical conditions. Ann had fibroid tumors which had evolved to a very dangerous stage and Monica found out she had uterine cancer which was spreading like wildfire. Both girls needed surgery, and fast. The girls asked their doctors if one could wait until she recovered from her surgery before the other had hers, but, both surgeons emphatically told them no. Monica and Ann went to the hospital in the same cab, Ann went to Bournemouth Hospital while Monica went to Poole Hospital, about 10 miles away. They were soon to find out that they were about to experience some hauntingly similar circumstances.

Monica feeling lots better.

Their surgery was scheduled for the same time the next day and they both came out of surgery at approximately the same time. Both Monica and Ann awoke from their anesthetic and asked how each other came through their surgeries. At the same time Monica's nurse phoned Ann's nurse, Ann's nurse was on another line to Monica's nurse. The girls both had music playing in their recovery room. When each nurse asked each other what song was currently playing, they both responded, "Please Don't Be Scared."

For days following her surgery, Monica was confined to a radiotherapy isolation room with only her tape player, a few photos and a VCR to help her pass the time. Barry Manilow was never far from her reach.

Monica and Ann have both recovered from their respective illnesses and they continue to grab life by the tail and live it to the fullest. They are certainly not going to let their health get in the way of following their "cheeky chappy" Barry.

The place: Chicago, Illinois.
The occasion: Barry Manilow Convention, 1983.
The goal: Make them laugh!

*Barbara Lovejoy of Murfreesboro*, Tennessee, and two of her Barry buddies decided to enter a talent contest, of sorts, in the comedy category offered as one of the activities during the convention. Barbara and her cronies burned up the phone lines between New York and Cleveland plotting and preparing for their performance. The theme of the skit was agreed upon; what if Barry was 77 and still touring? Hence, the title of their skit, "World Tour 2023." There would be three girls in the skit, two portraying aged Manilow fans, and one playing Barry's nurse. They rummaged through consignment shops looking for the appropriate attire; housedresses, knee highs, and plastic shopping bags. The two playing the older Manilow fans even grayed their hair for the skit.

One guess at who Barbara's favorite entertainer is.

The night before their debut, Barbara caught a head cold, which turned into bronchitis. She was losing her voice at break-neck speed. They were all so nervous, they taped the script inside one of the tour books they were using as props. Their moment had arrived and they breezed through the performance like pros. Some of their script included priceless prose such as when the nurse ran across the stage, Barbara's character yelled "Who was that?"

"Barry's nurse," replied her wilting white-haired partner. "He found her at 'the home' when he was sitting in a corner mumbling, 'I write the...I write the....'"

The nurse yelled, "Songs, you old coot!" They made references to the possibility that "Could It Be Magic" would have to be cut from his performance as he would fall asleep during the instrumental part of the song. One of Barbara's favorite portions of the act, being that she had not yet been chosen to sing "Can't Smile Without You" with Barry, was when her character remarked that after 40 years she was still waiting to be chosen.

Her concert buddy snapped back, "Well, he has to pick you soon, 'cause everyone else is dead!"

Much to their amazement, their skit won first prize in the comedy category and it wasn't until this past year that she found out that someone had videotaped the performance and sent it to Barry. Barbara was told that Barry enjoyed the performance very much. "If he hadn't laughed, I might be following Wayne Newton right now," confessed Barbara.

*You've heard the horror stories* many people tell about their experiences traveling by plane; missed flights, delays, turbulence and lost luggage to name a few.

Nancy Rosebrugh and her sister, Darlene, were traveling from California to Memphis, Tennessee, in 1997 to attend the Barry Manilow Convention when they fell victim to the luggage disaster. When they arrived in Memphis, their luggage didn't arrive with them. Nancy had dressed up for the flight wearing a pale peach linen pantsuit, gold shoes, and a fancy pin to complete her look. Nancy was looking chic but slightly overdressed as practically everybody else there for the convention festivities that afternoon was wearing shorts and T-shirts. Nancy ignored the fact that her attire was not "dress code," and proceeded to join the activities and socialized just the same.

Fortunately for Nancy, included in the convention welcome items was a Barry Manilow T-shirt. "All I had to wear to sleep that night was a Barry Manilow T-shirt we were given at the start of the convention, thank goodness," Nancy said

*As we get older,* we many times fall into our own patterns and habits of life. Perhaps we buckle down into an existence that includes taking fewer risks. Maybe we even tell ourselves that there are certain things we can no longer do, or do for the first time, because we are "too old for that." Shirley Beaird of Kirkwood, Missouri, refuses to limit herself in her golden years. In 1995, Shirley sold her home and moved into an apartment. There were many changes taking place in her life and this move seemed only logical. Shirley also had a gut feeling that she was going to get to see Barry Manilow in concert that year. She didn't know how she was going to get there and she had no idea where or when this would take place. But Shirley heeded to her inner voice and began looking at the options that would put her in the presence of Mr. Manilow himself.

Barry was touring that year so Shirley researched his concert schedule, checking on the ones closest to her home. She was too late to make arrangements for some and others required a bit too much coordination and costly hotel accommodations. That turned Shirley off from even trying to make it happen. Then Shirley found out about a six-show run in Las Vegas, Nevada. That made her ears perk up. She knew she couldn't afford to attend all six shows and pay for her travel and hotel room, so she settled on attending three shows.

Shirley contacted a travel agency in California that coordinates many package plans in conjunction with Barry's concert appearances, and began to make arrangements for the shows coming up in Las Vegas. The agency took care of her flight arrangements as well as coordinating her hotel stay. But what made Shirley's case different was that she didn't have a credit card number to give this agency for billing. Shirley didn't own a credit card. So on good faith and the honor system, Shirley promised to send them a check to cover her arrangements. The very day she phoned them, she wrote the check and mailed it off. Her dream was coming true.

Shirley had seen Barry in concert before, her first one taking place in 1993 and from the moment she heard his inspiring messages and words of wisdom that he shares with his audiences, she began to believe more in herself and her abilities. That trip to Las Vegas was proof that she had experienced a change. Before then she never would have thought she'd make it to Las Vegas, and travel there alone. "If it were not for Barry, I would never attempted to go to Las Vegas by myself," Shirley said. As it turned out, a pal from her local fan club, Manilow Music of Missouri, was able to attend the Vegas shows too. Shirley felt much better having a friend to spend her time with and share the fantastic concerts with, not that she would have had any trouble hooking up with a number of other folks there for the same reason.

"I'll never forget my Las Vegas trip," said Shirley "Barry inspires us so much with his musical talent and little messages, making us feel like family." Young and old, the Manilow family continues to grow.

*On March 7, 1984,* Marianne Felk's inner voice told her to record Barry Manilow's Blenheim Palace concert which appeared on television around midnight. When she returned home from work the next day Marianne watched the recorded show. "I could not believe what I saw, I could not believe what I heard," Marianne remembered. "I never heard anyone sing like this, I never saw an audience react like this. It was so amazing."

From that moment forward, Marianne had to find out who this Barry Manilow guy was. That was no simple task living in Berlin, Germany. She located a small Barry Manilow Fan Club and found a fan, Alexandra, also from Berlin. Alexandra began to introduce Marianne to other Manilow fans. In 1984, Marianne and Alexandra attended Barry's concert at Wembley Arena in London, England. They were in row "Z," but that didn't stop them from being completely taken by Barry's intimate approach on stage. They immediately took in two more shows at Wembley. Marianne and Alexandra had already decided they would start their own Barry Manilow Fan Club, so they contacted the Barry Manilow International Fan Club, UK, who helped them reach other German fans.

Marianne was hungry to learn more about Barry Manilow. After purchasing a few books about Barry, Marianne sat down with a dictionary and read every line of each book, translating as she went. Friends would also send her video copies of Barry's TV interviews. "Barry became my English teacher and I sound as if I come from Brooklyn," Marianne explained.

On several occasions Marianne has traveled to the states to visit Barry's old stomping grounds and to see him in concert. In 1987 Marianne traveled to Dallas, Texas, to spend Christmas with a pen pal she had met through following Barry's career. They went to Los Angeles to see Barry in concert at the Pentages. After the concerts, Marianne and her pals stood by the stage door to wave farewell to Barry. Marianne watched as she saw Barry hop into his car and drive away. She knew that Barry had learned how to drive later in life and witnessing Barry's independence that night inspired her. "Barry learned to drive a car, I would learn too. That's what I did," said Marianne. "I bought myself a little used car and practiced as much as I could. I had never wanted a car because I was scared of driving and always had thought it was too dangerous. Barry made me change my mind."

In 1993, the rubber hit the road and Marianne drove herself from Los Angeles to San Diego to see Barry in concert. "I was so proud of myself," said Marianne. And rightly so, as many people, let alone a person from Germany, might be reluctant to drive in California. "All I ever wanted was to be where he is and so I'm spending all my vacations at places where I can see Barry on stage," said Marianne. Since 1984 Marianne has seen Barry in concert over 185 times. She has been lucky enough to meet him on many occasions too.

But even more gratifying than a brief, passing meeting with Barry are the everlasting accomplishments Marianne has made in her life because of him. "I learned driving, I learned English, I've become an independent, self-confident person through all of this. I'm not afraid anymore to board a plane all by myself, rent a car and drive around," Marianne said.

"I don't wear T-shirts with Barry's face on it, I don't hold signs for 'Can't Smile Without You,'" Marianne explained. "I just go to the shows as often as I can, enjoy myself and thank God that He made me discover Barry. He's been the best thing that ever happened to me!"

*Have you ever experienced* something that so radically changed your life you wanted to share with the entire world how others could be eternally altered by the experience too? Franette Armstrong has.

In 1995, Franette traveled to Canada to undergo a vision correction procedure that had not yet been approved in the States. She was impressed by the results, not to mention elated by the fact that she would no longer require glasses. But, because of limited access to the facilities and doctors who performed this procedure, there was also limited information on the recovery process. "The experience was life changing, but I had absolutely no information to help me through the recovery period," said Franette. "I decided that I could write a book that would help others avoid some of the mistakes I made."

Although Franette is the founder and president of her own marketing agency, she is no stranger to writing. Franette has been writing some 20 years. She is also familiar with the book-writing process, having penned several works. But this subject is so personal to Franette, she put her business on hold not only to write the book, but to publish it, write and appear in a PBS special showcasing her book, and then to write a second edition of the book. The result of her labor of love is *Beyond Glasses! The Consumer's Guide to Laser Vision Correction*, a 396-page book describing in detail all of the permanent solutions available to people who are nearsighted, farsighted, have astigmatism or age-related reading visions problems.

To write the book, Franette interviewed all the doctors who developed the lasers and procedures, the manufacturers, and the 27 doctors in the U.S. and Canada who developed and tested the treatments through 10 years of clinical trials. Needless to say, this was a major undertaking for Franette. She interviewed experts from all over the globe which put her at the mercy of their varied and hectic schedules. But one day when she was conducting an interview with one of the contributors at UCLA's Jules Stein Eye Institute, Franette asked a question quite off the cuff that ultimately, significantly altered the course of her project.

Because that medical facility is situated in the "Land of the Stars," Franette asked if that doctor had corrected the vision of any famous people. The response she received could have knocked her over with a feather. "How would you like to interview Barry Manilow?" the doctor asked. Franette was thrilled.

After a lot of back-and-forth with his business manager and agent, Franette managed to conduct an interview by fax just as Barry was getting ready to leave for a London tour. "I was working around the clock to get the book out, so I sent him questions at the end of one day in April," Franette recalled. Much to her delight, Barry faxed the answers back to her the very next day. "I immediately wrote the story and faxed it to his home in the middle of the night," said Franette. "To my surprise, he faxed me back five minutes later!"

After the book's publication, Franette was contacted by the Denver PBS station and approached to adapt her book into a one-hour documentary. Eagerly, Franette accepted and "Beyond Glasses & Contacts!" was born. Upon agreeing to do this, Franette knew she wanted Barry to be involved in it too. She contacted Barry to see if he'd be willing to be interviewed as part of the PBS Special and when he said yes, she worked up the nerve to ask for his help in obtaining permissions to use music and/or videos of two of his songs, "It's a Miracle" and "Daybreak."

"Barry, along with his business manager, road manager, agent, and Arista Records, all bent over backwards to make all of this happen," said Franette. "Let me tell you, over a period of three months, the phone, voicemails and faxes filled a binder. The paper trail on the music rights and video rights alone took another binder; the music world is so complex. But it all works beautifully in the program."

One of the major challenges for Franette was finding a place for the interview with Barry to be taped. Barry was traveling the country on tour and she was traveling a different path to interview the leading doctors all over the country. Their schedules were so tight, there was no room for making changes. With her minimal PBS budget, she was not afforded the opportunity for a second trip to the East Coast to interview Barry and he wasn't due back out West until after her deadline. After much thought and creative planning, they agreed to meet in St. Louis at the amphitheater where Barry would be performing. PBS hired a contract crew to meet them at the amphitheater and all Franette had to do was show up by 12:30 PM.

The day of the interview, the combination of heavy, hard rain, thunder and lightning resulted in delayed flights. Franette's 8:00 AM flight didn't leave the ground until 11:00 AM! After landing, she waited for her luggage, hailed a cab, and made the half-hour trip to the amphitheater a panicked wreck. At the amphitheater, Barry's road manager greeted her and gave her a quick tour of the stage and then showed her to her dressing room. And what a dressing room she scored! "After doing wardrobe and makeup in hospital supply closets and doctor office bathrooms, I nearly wept with joy at having space to dress in and a decent mirror," Franette said. "The room was decorated like a hotel suite with air conditioning, a sofa, chair and coffee table, wall-to-wall mirrors surrounded with lights, a shower, and a basket of fruit!" She locked the door, did some yoga, took a quick shower, dressed and did her makeup and walked out just as Barry was entering the dressing room they would be using for the taping.

"When I first saw Barry, he was dressed in black jeans and a royal blue shirt over a white T-shirt," Franette remembered. "I was struck by two things: how tall he was and how tired he looked. He's extremely hand-some, as you know, but his eyes were ringed with fatigue circles." At that time, Barry was nearing the end of a four-month tour that involved a different hotel nearly every night. "Next," Franette said, "I was impressed by how gentle and non-egotistical he was." Months prior in preparation, it had been stressed that a video monitor be available for Barry to check the lighting and camera angles before the taping began. Franette readied the crew to spend some time setting up the scene to Barry's liking. "I assumed that Big Star equaled Big Ego," said Franette. "In actuality, we took our seats across from one another, Barry glanced at the monitor and suggested lowering the angle just a bit and then he was ready to go. There were no retakes."

Franette broke the interview into a couple of sets so they could change camera angles. During the first break Barry told her, "Franette, you're a natural at this! You could really do this for a living." All the nervousness that had built up from the moment he agreed to help her was immediately relieved and Franette felt more at ease. "In that one compliment," Franette said, "I felt I had seen into the heart of Barry Manilow; a gentle, generous star who would go out of his way to help make a total amateur look good."

They finished the interview, Franette taped a few more minutes of material for future editing into the interview and then she went to thank Barry. By that time, he had removed his blue shirt and was down to a T-shirt and jeans. "He has quite a physique, I must say," Franette admitted. He invited her to stay for that evening's concert, but she reluctantly had to decline because of a previous commitment. He gave her a big hug for the camera and it was a wrap.

Well, if Franette wasn't a fan of Barry's before her encounter with him, she sure is now. "I have all of his CDs and I know most of his songs by heart. Now, of course, I eagerly read every bit of news I can get on him," she said. Unfortunately, though, she has not been able to make it to his concerts. Surely, that will change too. There is nothing quite like seeing this, as Franette described, "warm" and "personable" fellow in action!

Would you, too, like to live life without the hassles of wearing glasses? Why don't you inquire about the procedure that corrected Franette and Barry's impaired vision. Here's how:

*Beyond Glasses! The Consumer's Guide to Laser Vision Correction,* by Franette Armstrong with an introduction by James J. Salz, MD (396-page book) is $19.95 (ISBN 0-9656505-0-2). "Beyond Glasses & Contacts!" (56 min. PBS special on videocassette) is $24.95. Purchase them together for $39.95, a 10% savings.

Website: http://www.beyondglasses.com
E-mail orders: ucbooks@aol.com
Tollfree orders: 888-411-2075 (VISA, MC, Amex)
Fax orders: 925-820-3711
Mail orders: UC Books, Box 1036, Danville, CA 94526

*When ordering, mention that you read Franette's story in *The Whole World Sings: The fans behind Barry Manilow*, and receive a 20% discount!

Taken in the parking lot at Wembley London in January of 1998.
This is the back of the Maniloonie Tour Bus that followed Barry from one concert
stop to the next.

# Chapter Three

# I Was A Fool:
# Barry Blunders

Whether you have followed Barry Manilow's career since the beginning or you have just discovered him, sooner or later, you will most likely fall victim to a "Barry blunder." Traveling to concerts, CD signings, personal appearances or even e-mailing your Barry Buddies affords fans plenty of opportunities for some funny experiences. Whether you are a major admirer of Barry Manilow or a closet fan, you will chuckle as you read the next stories. These fans have traversed the globe and traveled across town to see Barry and to interact with their pals. What transpired on some of these trips created indelible memories for these fans.

These stories are not intended for us to laugh at these folks, rather, we should laugh with these brave souls who told their tales. Really, how many of you would repeat some of your most embarrassing moments for a book? Any one of these experiences could have easily happened to any one of us; and it did. You'll read one of my very own "Barry Blunders."

Enjoy a good laugh as you read these stories but remember, the next time…the blooper could be yours!

**"Whenever I think of Barry Manilow,** the first song that comes to mind is 'Could It Be Magic,'" said Leslie Millsap. Leslie is so fond of the song that whenever she is out on the town and frequents a piano bar, she always requests it.

One evening, Leslie and her mother were dining at an elegant restaurant in Boston. Upon being seated, Leslie almost immediately noticed a handsome, young man, (who was wearing a white tuxedo, and playing masterfully at a beautiful grand piano.) She noticed an elegant glass sitting atop the piano where patrons had generously added crisp bills throughout the evening. When Leslie finally worked up the nerve, she arose from her chair and proceeded toward the piano player to make her request. Leslie was looking exceptionally good that night as she shimmied through the crowd in her mini skirt.

From the pedestal where the piano was, the young musician looked down at Leslie and asked her what she would like to hear. She placed her dollar bill in his glass and sheepishly whispered, "Could you please play 'Could It Be Magic' by Barry Manilow?" He flashed Leslie a big grin and said, "Hey, you want to hear Barry Manilow, you get Barry Manilow." Before she even completely descended from the upper level, the familiar chords of the Chopin "Prelude" began to tango with the light conversation and the pings of forks and knives touching china. Leslie returned to her seat to witness one of the most beautiful renditions of "Magic" that she had ever heard. Leslie looked around the restaurant to find practically every eye fixated on the piano man.

Finally, the young talent concluded the song quite dramatically, careful to include the soft, poignant last notes, played to perfection. You could have heard a pin drop. The entire restaurant stood to their feet and gave him a well-deserved and enthusiastic round of applause. He took a few bows, then excused himself for a break.

Leslie turned her attention back to her mother and her dinner when suddenly she noticed the piano player approaching their table. He bent down beside Leslie, looked straight into her eyes and said, "How was I? Any good?" Leslie's mind raced for all the right words. "Good" just didn't seem adequate. They exchanged a few words and then he explained how he had learned the song when he was in high school. "Thanks a lot, kid," flooded her thoughts.

Leslie's striking appearance had most likely led the young piano player to believe that she was nearer to his age than her actual age. This honest mistake happens all the time to Leslie, which certainly doesn't bother her.

*A career as a professional* photographer meant that Debbie Cohen of Pittsburgh, Pennsylvania, went to Barry's concerts well equipped with camera, tripod, lens, and plenty of film. Her efforts were rewarded with great shots, some of which decorate her home game room. When Barry was appearing in Atlantic City, New Jersey, for a few days, Debbie decided to send one of her original photographs to Barry for an autograph. She recalls spending a "small fortune" on overnight postage for this picture, a pen, and a self addressed stamped envelope, which was a small price to pay for a signature. Her poor postman almost got tackled when he delivered the return parcel. Imagine Debbie's disappointment when she ripped open the envelope to find her picture and pen, just the way she sent them, with no autograph.

*As a Training Specialist* for the Department of Social Services, Jill Prince wears many hats during a typical day. But, when Barry is on tour, Jill and a group of friends normally take much deserved vacation time (and a little personal time, too) to visit a variety of cities, both in the States and abroad, to see Barry's shows. On one day in April, 1997, Jill skillfully donned another hat as she played New York City tour guide to a huge group of fans while they visited the city for Barry's Radio City Music Hall run.

Jill has traveled to many states and has seen a number of Barry's concerts in her day – upwards of the 75 mark since her first show in 1984. Jill has stood along-side Sally Jesse Raphael as an audience member chosen to speak to Sally's special guest, Barry Manilow, she has been interviewed by Al Roker of *The Today Show* when Barry appeared there during the 1997 Summer Concert Series, she has had several up close and personal encounters with Barry throughout the years, and to top it all off, Jill was even chosen to sing "Can't Smile Without You" with Barry in 1997. Needless to say, Jill has racked up some fabulous memories following Barry Manilow's career. But, one moment stands out in Jill's mind as being among the funniest things she ever witnessed.

That moment was when the group of fans she was hosting wanted to take a ride on the famous Staten Island Ferry.

As the Statue of Liberty came into view, the group didn't want this monumental moment to pass them by, for perhaps they would never get the opportunity to see this historical landmark again. Jill, having seen the Statue a hundred times before, humored the group and watched them step out on the deck of the Ferry to brave the cold, rainy, windy, absolutely miserable day for a peek at the illustrious statue. Jill chose to remain inside where it was warm and flipped through the newspaper. As the gals oohed and ahhed their way into the mist, they neglected to shut the door to the cabin behind them.

There it was, standing before them, steeped in rich history...the Statue of Liberty. For this group visiting New York City for Barry Manilow's concerts, the emotions ran high. Actually, as if something inside of them snapped, in unison, they began tapping their toes to a tune.

Because of the forceful winds and rain, conversation was labored. They practically had to yell at each other to hear what the other was saying. So, when that tune transformed from a toe-tap into a burst of vocal splendor, the gals had to sing rather loudly to hear each other. After all, it was important that their harmonies were on key and that they were in the proper timing. But, what fell from their lips was not a Barry Manilow song, as one might expect. They had a more appropriate melody to mark the occasion with. This group became inhabited by the spirit of Barbra Streisand and in sweet southern accents, they performed their best rendition of "Don't Rain On My Parade."

The open door to the cabin provided commuters inside with the serenade. "I was almost hysterical watching the faces of the commuters as this was going on," recalls Jill.

The group ended their tribute with grins and giggles and returned to the cabin to join Jill. Jill fiddled with her newspaper and commented on the beautiful homage. Unable to control herself any longer, Jill informed the choral group of their performance to the Ferry passengers. The group had no idea that their voices had carried into the confines of the cabin.

In attempts to smooth over the awkward situation, one member of the group told a man who glanced up from his paper at the famous group, "We're from out of town." The man replied, "I never would've guessed."

*Following some rough times*, Stella Capp of Manchester, England, was overdue for better days, but little did she realize that Barry would be a part of those better days. At the time in 1994 when Stella was pulling herself through, Barry was in the process of getting the musical *Copacabana* up and running in Britain. When it was scheduled to play at the Prince of Wales Theatre in London's West End, a radio station ran a promotion offering not only a trip to London including two show tickets but passes to the celebrity party following the show. Stella had been following Barry's musical career since 1977 and not surprisingly, she entered the contest in her name and also in the name of her daughter, Clare, who was eleven at the time. Lady Luck shined on the Capp family when the young girl was selected the contest's grand prize winner.

Clare remained calm as Stella reeled from the excitement and fast moving agenda. The wheels were put into motion as the adventure began with a VIP rail trip from Manchester to London, followed by a limo ride to their suite at London's Hilton Hotel. As she dressed for the evening's performance, Stella tried not to conjure up false hopes of actually meeting

Barry. However, these thoughts were simmering in the back of her mind as she and Clare were escorted into the stage door of the theatre and took in the sights and sounds of all the props, costumes, and scenery. Soon they were chatting with star of the show, Gary Wilmot, and then it was on to their seats in time for the opening curtain. They savored every moment of the performance, but, of course, Barry was the highlight in their eyes. The finale received a long, standing ovation, but when Barry walked on stage, the crowd shrieked and clapped even more. Barry graciously thanked those involved with the production for its overwhelming success. As they clapped and he left the stage, Stella and Clare didn't realize that the best was yet to be.

Stella and Clare hurriedly exited in hopes of seeing Barry leave the theatre. There he was sitting in his limo, ready to go. But their limo had his limo blocked in. (To this day, Stella adamantly denies arranging this delay.) After arriving at the Copa Party back at the Hilton, the contest winners found that their luck was still with them. The party room included spectacular decorations and a band playing show tunes. Their table was near the dance floor and their dinner companions were executives from the radio station that sponsored the contest. As Stella and Clare tried to absorb all the sights and sounds of the moment for their memory banks, the band played "Copacabana" and everyone stood up. They also rose, but didn't realize why until a spotlight hit the door and in walked Barry Manilow. He casually took a seat at his table, which was just across the dance floor from them. Now Stella and Clare had to eat a meal in full view of Barry.

Soon Roger Holdom, a marketing manager for Radio 2, appeared between Clare and Stella and said, "Right, you're coming with me, he'll see you now." As Clare remained cool, calm and collected, Stella's jaw hit the floor when she was introduced to Barry and he took her hand. They told him how much they enjoyed the show and he posed for pictures with Clare. In parting, Stella told Barry that she would see him perform live again in a few months and thought her Barry encounters were over for the evening. But she was wrong. The most personal experience was yet to come.

After chatting with friends, Stella and Clare had to weave around the darkened dance floor to return to their table. They were holding hands as they navigated when Stella's hand brushed across someone's backside. She looked up to apologize, when she saw the back of Barry's head as he turned and smiled at Clare. She'd brushed Barry's behind, even if it was an accident, and Clare was getting all the credit. At a momentary loss for words, Stella meekly took her seat. Clever replies came to her much later. But the moment had passed without a peep from Stella.

A wonderful evening ended when Barry left the party and the Capps returned to their suite, drifting off to sleep with about 50 helium "Copa" balloons from the party floating overhead.

Clare and Barry at the Copa Party.

*Atlantic City, New Jersey*, was the location of another blooper, this time by Carrie Diener of Beltsville, Maryland, and Linda Brubaker of Rockville, Maryland. While walking back to their hotel after Barry's concert, Carrie was thrilled to recognize one of the three men approaching them as Barry's assistant, Marc Hulett. "Great show, Marc," she replied and Marc thanked her as the men strolled past. Carrie was basking in the moment when Linda abruptly put an end to her pleasure saying, "You just passed Barry and didn't say a word."

Of course, the men were gone when she recovered enough to turn around. She had missed her chance to speak to Barry.

The moral of this story is: wherever Marc Hulett is, Barry may not be far away.

*Hilarious bloopers can take* place at any time, anywhere. Patricia Loram of Bristol, England, attended Barry's concert in Cardiff with two "Barry Buddies," Kathy and Carole. In order to provide three beds, their hotel added a fold away bed to their room. Patricia raced from the bathroom when Carole, hysterical with laughter, called her. She was greeted with a most unusual view of Kathy, who had her head sticking out from one side of the extra bed, while her feet dangled from the other side. It seemed Kathy's attempt to sit up in the middle of her bed had caused the fold up mechanism to activate. Sadly, Patricia's camera was out of film, so this didn't get recorded.

*What would you do* if you had paid for airplane tickets and a hotel room for a Manilow convention and your boss said he couldn't spare you from work? How about scheduling surgery in order to get medical leave? That's what Toni Josleyn from Merrillville, Indiana, did just before Convention '96. When she was unable to get away from her job as a school bus driver at the start of the school year, she phoned her physician to schedule some needed minor elective surgery. If everything had gone according to her plans, her two week medical leave would have been divided between a week at home recuperating followed by a week at the convention.

But, of course, these well made plans didn't fall into place. Her surgeon rescheduled the surgery for the day before she was leaving for the convention. Fortunately, Toni breezed through the surgery. She made her flight and recuperated, with the help of pain pills, in the hot Las Vegas sun. "This was the first time we were going to be there for the whole run at the Mirage and there was no way I was going to miss it," explained Toni. "We had the time of our lives."

Fortunately, Toni still had a week at home after the concerts for some much needed rest before she returned to work.

*Jean Phillips of South* Gloucestershire, England, enjoyed the musical *Copacabana* so much she had to purchase the soundtrack. According to Jean, the only way to properly appreciate the recording is playing it loud.

One day while vacuuming, Jean put the *Copa* CD on and before long, "Bolero De Amour" began to play. This dramatic piece of music called for exaggerated sweeping movements and Jean, alone (or so she thought), became swept up in the moment, and caught herself singing at the top of her lungs. Getting that strange feeling that she was being watched, Jean looked up to find a very amused window cleaner. "But, who cares!" said Jean.

*If given the choice* between working and seeing Barry live and in person, what would you do? Probably, exactly what Christine Smith of

West Midlands, England, did when Barry appeared at Pebble Mill in Birmingham, England. Of course, Christine wanted to be a part of the action. It was almost impossible to get time off from her job as a dinner lady in a school. So Christine told her supervisor what she calls a "little white Barry lie," which are those tall tales used only when absolutely needed in order to see Barry in person. Instead of going to the hospital with her mother, which was the "Barry lie," she went to the TV studio and waited for Barry to arrive.

During the program, Barry thrilled Christine and the crowd by waving at them through the window. Her thrills turned to chills when she realized that she had been filmed, along with the rest of the crowd, and the TV station planned to air their footage the next morning.

"I was scared stiff to go in to work the next day, but, miraculously, nobody saw me," Christine sighed. "It was worth it anyway."

♪♪♪♪♪

*By far, the best* part about writing this book has been the wonderful opportunities I've had to meet Barry's fans. These awesome fans have been eager to enhance my limited knowledge about the "Manilow moments" before, during, and after his concerts. Their generosity included not only sharing their special stories but also providing me with video tapes of their "Can't Smile Without You" duets with Manilow and a variety of his past TV performances. This caring relationship also led to my big blooper.

Months before, my VCR had been programmed to record a cooking show where chefs from around the world show off their expertise in food preparation and presentation.

Ann Underwood of L.O.V.E. Barry Manilow Fan Club (BMFC) in Milwaukee, Wisconsin sent me a tape of past TV appearances, which included Manilow's visit with Suzanne Somers on her talk show, and his *Larry King Live* visit where he performed selections from "Singing With the Big Bands." A note from Ann stated that she wanted me to make my own copy of her tape and return hers when I was finished with it. Ann had entrusted me, a virtual stranger, with the care and safe return of one of her prized possessions.

As soon as I received it, I immediately popped Ann's tape into my VCR. I saw the emotion shared between good friends as Barry and Suzanne Somers shared details of their lives with their television audience. I witnessed Barry practically cause a meltdown in the microphone on *Larry King Live* as he sang Big Band tunes and enlightened his viewers about the story behind each song. There was so much on the tape, I couldn't watch it all at one time. I had work to do.

Hours later, I heard one of life's most annoying sounds coming from my living room. As I followed the trail toward the offending sound, it registered in my brain what I was hearing. The culprit was the buzz of a VCR tape. Sheer panic set in. Ann's tape! I raced to my entertainment center, which requires an engineering degree with a minor in programming to operate the on/off switch. The television alone is the size of Montana, and the whole center has enough wires to operate the space shuttle.

In a real panic, I reached the VCR and hit the STOP button. Nothing happened. More vigorously, I punched EJECT. Nothing ejected. I repeatedly hit STOP and EJECT with a speed and precision that would make any drummer proud.

Now what? Go for the wires! I chased the main wire to my wall plug and pulled. My electric meter must have whirled to a crawl as my electronic marvel shut down. Hidden behind my television, I slumped on the floor in total exhaustion. Even though this episode took only a few seconds, the mental anguish was overwhelming.

The moment of truth was not far away when I placed the plug back into the wall socket. I had a pretty good idea of what had happened, but the damage was yet to be assessed. I pushed REWIND and began to pray. No kidding. When I pressed PLAY I was greeted with a Montana-size view of a man sporting a white chef coat and a tall, white cap with a raw chicken in his hand. He was quite eloquent in explaining how he would separate the wings, legs, etc.

I forwarded the tape to find that this raw chicken had rudely interrupted an intimate conversation between Barry and Suzanne Somers. Somewhat recovered, my wheels started turning. I had another copy of that interview on another tape, so I could simply record over the "foul" parts, and Ann's tape would be good as new. What a clever idea. Well, the two tapes were recorded on different speeds and when I viewed Ann's "corrected" tape, I was once again privy to the insides of a raw bird.

The moment of truth had arrived. It was time to "fess up" to Ann. I remorsefully sent her an e-mail explaining every detail, assuring her that I would do whatever was necessary to make up for my bird-brain mistake. Little did I know that Ann sent me her backup tape, not the only copy she possessed of these television performances. You would be hard pressed to find a fan who does not have multiple copies of his or her Barry tapes. Obsessive? No, smart! Manilow fans take pleasure from sharing tapes with others who enjoy them and one can never be sure what will happen to them once they leave the secure clutches of their owners.

The moral of this story, and there is one: share your copied tapes of Barry's TV appearances with your friends.

# *Chapter Four*

# "Can't Smile Without You"

I n our lives we are all given opportunities that, once experienced, change us forever. For many Manilow fans, the quintessential moment is being chosen to sing Barry's "Can't Smile Without You" on stage with him. Here's how it works.

Sometime during the concert, the band begins to play that familiar tune and a frenzy envelopes the audience. Anybody who has been to at least one Manilow concert knows what is about to take place. All of a sudden, home-made signs begin popping up from under chairs and behind rows of seats. A wave of multi-colored paperboard floods the venue. Each sign bears a phrase that, with a little creativity and a lot of luck, Barry will read and invite the sign-holder to be the next CSWY participant. Some fans simply begin to jump up and down and wave their hands, some stand on their chairs, calling out for Barry's attention. Others strategically plan their clothing for this event, all in attempts to catch the eye of the man they want to get close to.

How about a few minutes of singing with Barry Manilow? Or maybe a little soft shoe with Barry Manilow? Perhaps the opportunity to hug Barry, hold his hand and receive a parting kiss as you leave the stage? Any of those would be great, wouldn't they? The CSWY participants get them all plus a VCR tape of their performance autographed by Barry himself. Most of all, these fans leave the concert with a memory that they will keep forever.

It is an honor to be chosen for this moment and subsequently to be initiated into this exclusive club. Although every CSWY experience is different, Barry conducts their performance with precision and accuracy so each person who graces the stage not only knows what to expect, but is carefully guided through the experience. The one who should be a bit nervous is Barry! In his years of inviting these gals to duet with him, he has encountered a variety of personalities. Really, what would you do if all of a sudden, you found yourself on stage with Barry Manilow? Although most are able to keep their composure and belt out a recognizable rendition of this most popular tune, some close encounters are of the reckless kind. Even Barry himself tells of the time one excited fan momentarily lost control of her bladder on stage. That is a rare occurrence. Most of the fans, although stunned virtually stiff and flabbergasted that they were chosen, are gracious.

You are about to read a few stories of the hundreds of CSWY girls. Every one has a unique story with her own speculations as to why she was chosen for this monumental event. Is there a science for being chosen to sing with Barry? Some believe there are a few common denominators that scream "Can't Smile." You be the judge as you read through these miraculous moments.

*"Over the course of* time, I've had a lot of personal challenges. I knew I could always count on the

feelings I got and the friends I had through Barry. It was something that I wanted to do. People who know me know that I don't do this. I don't like to call attention to myself. I get very nervous other than talking one-on-one to somebody. I think I'm personable enough, I just don't like to be the center of attention. However, the only way that I was ever going to get up on that stage was to be the center of attention. Barry had said something a while back that stated that nobody is going to make things happen for you unless you do it yourself and nobody wants things more than you do, so, you've got to go out and get them. I decided that we have been so blessed and so lucky to have Barry around, active in a career and performing throughout the country so much, how much longer is this going to go on? So, I decided I was going to do it, and I did," said Darlene Schwartz. What did she do? She became a "Can't Smile Without You" girl, of course.

If you have ever attended a Manilow concert, you probably noticed during the preparation for Barry's performance of "Can't Smile Without You," signs of all shapes and sizes, colors and slogans pop up all over the venue. Fans hoping to be chosen by Barry to sing this song with him carefully design their signs hoping these clever cardboard (and sometimes cloth) masterpieces will land them a spot on the stage. For five of a six night run at the Mirage in Las Vegas, Darlene of Northbrook, Illinois, used a sign that got her absolutely nowhere. The night after the fifth show, Darlene was awakened out of her sleep with a premonition to change her sign. Leaving nothing to chance, Darlene went out the next day and bought the materials to make her new sign.

Fashioned in the shape of a pig, this sign boasted the slogan, "I WANT YOU BABE!" Darlene is a collector of pig paraphernalia and she heard rumor that Barry's favorite movie at the time was *Babe*. "It was just too perfect," Darlene said.

According to Darlene, Barry scanned the audience, went to Darlene's side of the stage and said, "What does that sign say? 'I Want You Babe!' How can I resist?" Before she knew it, a member of Barry's staff was escorting her to the stage.

"I don't even know what I did, I did not know what I said until I got home and saw the video. I could not believe what came out of my mouth. How embarrassing! I had no clue. And, you don't care. You are up there and he is so calming and so take-charge that you don't really care," said Darlene. "I know that people were going to laugh, but, what did I care? So they'll have a good laugh, big deal! I'll go on with my life."

So, there she was, on stage with Barry Manilow. Was she worried about forgetting the lyrics to the song? No, she was more concerned with what he smelled like! "I had check points in my mind that if I ever get up on stage, these are the things that I want to do: I want to know what he smells like, I want to know what he feels like, I want to see his hair, I want to see his eyes. After the first checkpoint, when I first smelled him, forget it, I just lost it. What's going to happen will happen because I don't remember what I'm suppose to do," Darlene laughed.

So, what did he smell like? "Nothing," Darlene said. "He smelled clean."

Her moment ended, she was escorted back to her seat, and she stood as Barry finished singing the song. She jumped up and down and gave long-time Barry buddy, Laura Conners a huge bear-hug. It was over and she now has the video and the memories. "I was just proud of myself that I did it," recalled Darlene. "I was ready, and I wanted it."

"If you really want something bad enough and you strive for it, it can be achieved. I'm not going to say that it always will be achieved, but, it can be," stated Darlene.

Darlene Schwartz waves at friends.

*Barbara Lovejoy was tired.* She was making final preparations for her upcoming move to Murfreesboro, Tennessee, from Florida. Within this same week in December, 1997, Barry was performing in Fort Lauderdale and Tampa. Barbara was determined not to let her impending move stifle her opportunity to see Barry in concert. Even if she was dead tired, she was going to drive the 200 miles each way from her current home to the Fort Lauderdale concerts. Distance was not going to hinder Barbara; she was on a mission.

After seeing Barry's performances in Fort Lauderdale and attending the first of two nights in Tampa, Barbara was resigned to the fact that she would not be chosen to sing "Can't Smile Without You" with Barry on this tour. In her desperation, she even wrote Barry after the Fort Lauderdale concerts telling him that she "thought it was about time (to be chosen) since I wasn't getting any younger and would prefer to be picked while I still remembered the words to the song and could remember who he was." She also told Barry that she would be wearing red at the concerts until she was chosen. This might seem like a bold step to take, but, for Barbara, it is a familiar routine. Barbara regularly writes to Barry and jokingly calls him her "therapist."

The second night in Tampa, Barbara arrived at the venue sporting her red sweatshirt. Her pal, Pam, kept telling Barbara that she could feel that she was going to be picked. "Yeah, whatever," replied Barbara.

After intermission, the familiar sounds of "Can't Smile" began. The video began to play on the huge overhead screen on stage and women started shuffling around in their seats preparing for their big chance. Barbara turned to Pam and said, "Does my lipstick look all right?" Then she said, "I'm standing on the seat, it's now or never." Barry made his appearance on the stage belting out that familiar tune. The house came up and Barry asked for volunteers to sing with him. As Barbara stood on her seat, Pam held her hand so she wouldn't make a performance of another sort. "How about you in the red sweatshirt jumping up and down," Barbara remembers Barry saying. Barbara flew off her seat into the capable hands of the stage manager and he walked her to the stage from eleven rows back.

Barbara found herself face to face with Barry and all she remembers was saying, "Oh, my God, Oh, my God!" She remembers his gorgeous blue eyes and never wanting to stop hugging him. When asked what she does for work, Barbara was all set for her response. Let's face it, she has had plenty of time to rehearse. She told Barry that she is a critical care nurse and she majored in mouth-to-mouth resuscitation. The audience roared with laughter and Barry was quick to respond to her surmising that she had that answer all thought out.

The best moment for Barbara came when Barry turned to the audience and told them that Barbara is an "old fan friend of his." All of those years of letters, needlepoints, T-shirts, etc. paid off. Barry remembered her! That statement meant more to her than anything as it proved to her that Barry had read her mail and knows his fans, especially the fans that have been with him since the beginning. "Afterwards, everything was a blur. I don't remember much, Barry has that effect on women. I know it was only 5 minutes 37 seconds, but I will cherish it forever," Barbara remarked.

*The summer of '78* was very important to Christina Cotsifas. She was just 12 years old and she saw Barry Manilow in concert for her first time. She remembers hearing "Mandy" on the radio but it was "Weekend In New England" that really set her sails toward a life-long love of Barry's music. Over the years, Christina has racked up some awesome Manilow memories. She has seen him in concert over 70 times and during one of these concerts, she realized the dream she most coveted; she became a "Can't Smile" girl.

Her big day came on September 4, 1993, but her story really began on September 1st. It was a Wednesday and that evening Christina and four of her Barry Buddies attended Barry's concert in Allentown, Pennsylvania, not far from Christina's home in Coatsville, Pennsylvania. Some of her friends had better seats than the rest of the group, and unfortunately, Christina's seat was not one of the better ones. Fortunately, Christina packed her binoculars. During the entire show, Christina kept telling her friend that she had to see Barry in Atlantic City that Saturday evening. But there was a small problem. She didn't have tickets for the show.

The next day at work, she signed on to America Online (AOL) and posted a message that she was looking for a ticket for Barry's performance in Atlantic City on Saturday night. Not one hour later, Christina's plea was answered. Michael, Christina's new angel, sent an instant message telling her he had an extra ticket. Christina agreed to take the ticket and told Michael she'd meet him at 5:00PM, Saturday night to pick it up.

Christina now had two days to prepare for this Atlantic City concert she was obsessing over. For some reason, she knew she just had to be there. Before Christina set out on her road trip, she stopped at the local grocery store to buy supplies to make a poster. She settled on the bright florescent orange poster board and headed to the check out. Before she could reach the cashier, a man approached Christina and began complementing her on her dress and he told her how pretty she was. "I was trying to ignore him," Christina said, "as I was in a hurry. But I acted nice, thanked him, and left." Christina was over that obstacle, or so she thought. Out in the parking lot, Christina's new admirer came up to her and presented her with two yellow roses. "Now, I have never had a strange man bring me anything, so, I laughed to myself, got in the car, and flew to Atlantic City," recalled Christina.

The entire drive to AC, Christina's mind was racing with a myriad of thoughts, including what to write on the sign. She decided to ditch the sign she used for Barry's "Showstoppers" tour, as it got her nowhere. Before she knew it, she was wheeling into Atlantic City. She pulled into the casino parking lot, drove to the third level and there was a vacant parking spot! Imagine that. She met with Michael, got her ticket then proceeded to the ladies room to put her face on. When she emerged, she kept getting looks from people eyeing her.

Christina and Michael found their seats; dead center, half way back at the end of a table. They put their names on the "please move us list" and Christina decided it was high time to whip out her marker and make her sign. Everyone at her table was chuckling over Christina's sign-making timing. She made a huge "I" then under that, she drew a frowning smiley face with tears running from its eyes, representing "I Can't Smile."

When the CSWY song began playing, Christina found that for the first time in her life, she was able to whistle the entire whistling part. During the part where Barry asks for volunteers to sing with him, Christina raised her sign high. An usher came from nowhere and asked Christina to put her sign down. Christina was livid. Christina was so mad that not only did she hold her sign up again, when the house lights came up, she stood up and waved her sign with every ounce of might she had in her. Barry spotted the big "I" on the fluorescent orange sign and called Christina to the stage.

Christina always told herself that when she was chosen, she would have fun with the moment. She was shaking as she approached the stage. As she passed the rows of tables, her friends who were seated on the aisles smiled at Christina and touched her as she passed them, giving her the reassurance that she could do it. Christina took a couple of deep breaths, then took Barry's hand as he offered it to her and carefully climbed the few steps up to the stage. Then, she saw Barry's eyes. "I locked my gaze on his blue eyes! I tell you, I was mesmerized. No other word for it. I know my eyes must have been wide and my mouth wide open. For this man I was beholding in front of me was Barry Manilow. This gorgeous man!!" said Christina.

As if singing with Barry wasn't good enough, when Christina's shining moment was finished, she descended the steps from the stage to be greeted by Michael telling her that their seats had been changed to front and center.

One of the reasons why Christina's CSWY experience is so dear to her is because she was able to share her moment with her friends. "The great thing about having friends in the audience," Christina said, "is they tell you stuff you didn't even recall happening! It was wonderful to have all my friends there. You guys made it even more special and I was lucky to have you all there to witness my special night. I wouldn't have had it any other way. Michael, thanks for the ticket and putting up with a very excited woman!"

Christina's journey to "Can't Smile" took 11 years, but, it was worth the wait. "11 years," Christina said, "but it could not have happened at a better time in my life. I love you Barry, you are the best!!"

*May 30, 1997*, is a day that will live in infamy for Ann Underwood of Milwaukee, Wisconsin. Her special place was the Rosemont Theatre in Chicago, Illinois. Ann's "Can't Smile" story is not unlike the many other gals who are chosen.

Just in case you were curious about how she caught Barry's eye that evening, the sign she took said, "PLEASE PICK ME!" (Ann is very polite, after all). But, more than likely, the "dynamic duo" that did it for Ann that evening was the combination of her sign and the red jacket she was wearing. According to Ann, when Barry finally made his selection that evening, he called her from the audience by saying, "You, in the aisle in the red jacket and the sign that says, 'Please Pick Me.'"

Ann's performance was no less dynamic as she had prepared for that moment for many years. Just how does one prepare to sing with Barry Manilow? For Ann, she played and re-played the sequence of the CSWY segment in her mind until she had it memorized. Also, driving to and from work, she had logged many miles alone with Barry in her car, via his CDs, of course. She knew the song by heart. So, intellectually, she felt prepared for their meeting, not to mention the fact that being close to Barry was extremely appealing, too.

Her performance went off without a hitch and the meeting was even better than she ever imagined. She held his hand, sang & danced, and he cradled her between his legs as he sat on the piano during that famous moment relished by all CSWY gals. And before he let her go from the stage, Ann got her kiss from Barry too. Her reflexes took over and as he was still holding her right hand, her left hand sprang up to caress his face and hair. She was then escorted back to her seat for the rest of the show.

Although practically every female Manilow fan knows and desires the routine, Ann gets a charge out of some of the questions she has since been asked after her debut with Barry Manilow. Other than the standard, "What was it like?", a couple of the most memorable questions that folks have asked Ann include, "How does he smell?" (apparently many gals want to know this) and "Were his eyes bloodshot?" Go figure.

Even though Ann's CSWY moment ranks right up there with one of the most glorious experiences that has ever happened to her, she did mention that there were a few downsides to her moment. According to Ann, she lists them as follows:

1.  Sure is hard to concentrate on the rest of the show.
2.  No pictures.
3.  No sound on my video. (She was given an audio tape and has had it dubbed.)
4.  NO PICTURES!
5.  The clueless guy who appeared beside me just as the Can't Smile set started and said, 'Put that sign down and leave it down for the remainder of the show or you will be ejected from the theatre.' I waited for Barry to ask if anyone wanted to do this (be a CSWY girl), leapt to my feet and stood in the aisle with my sign. The rest is history. Note: Clueless guy came up to me later and apologized.
6.  NO PICTURES!
7.  My daughter, Heidi, wasn't there.

To those gals who want to be a CSWY girl but are a bit shy to try, Ann has some advice for you. "Don't be afraid. Barry is in total control. He knows you're star struck, nervous, and in love, on cloud nine, and he's watching you closely. He's gently but firmly leading you every moment. The crowd is friendly; Barry's people are super. It was a tremendous experience that I'll never forget. Thanks, Barry, I love you!!"

*By: Linda Phillips*
*Hazelwood, Missouri*


*June 16, 1989*
*Dear Diary,*

You could say that this has been one of the most wonderful days of my life! As you know, the whole time we planned this trip to Las Vegas, everybody hoped that someone we knew would get picked for "Can't Smile." I never thought that I would ever get picked though, because let's face it, I'm too short.

Our seats for the show were fantastic…about fifth or sixth from the stage. Mary V. and Harriet sat opposite Dianne and myself. When Barry started that familiar whistle, we squealed with anticipation. All the ladies around me started standing in the aisle. "Hmmm," I thought. "He'll never see me!" So, I stood on my chair. Barry said, "I want someone who really wants to do this." I clasped my hands pleadingly as Barry looked directly at our table. "What about you right there, this blonde right here," Barry said. I looked around for this lucky lady until I realized that he was talking about me. Amazed, I pointed to myself in disbelief! "Yes," Barry said. "You with the glasses on. Come on, darlin'."

I gracefully jumped off my chair, losing my shoe in the process. All sorts of thoughts raced through my mind as I frantically searched for my shoe. "Oh, my gosh, this is what I've dreamed of ever since I became a Barry Manilow fan! How many people are there in this audience. I must be CRAZY. What am I going to do if I can't find my shoe?" Luckily, I found the shoe without too much trouble.

Barry met me at the top of the stairs and he took my hand. His hands are very large and strong. "Look at you, you little thing, you," Barry said. This struck me as really funny because I had been thinking, "My goodness, is he tall!" Barry looked at me and said, "Gosh, you're pretty." Any composure I had managed suddenly went down the tubes. Barry started asking me questions, but, I'll be honest, when he looked at me with his beautiful baby blues, I found it difficult to concentrate on much else.

Barry went around to the back of the piano to get the second microphone and I took the opportunity to wave to my favorite Uncle. Then Barry and I started our fabulous duet. The whole time I thought, "This is truly a once-in-a-lifetime opportunity. I am really singing with Barry Manilow!" All too soon, our fantastic duet was over. Barry said, "You did great! Give me a hug." Now, how could I possibly deny a request like that? I put my arms around Barry's neck and he literally lifted me off the ground. In Barry's ear I whispered, "Thank you, Barry. Thank you so much!"

He escorted me to the stairs and we shared a quick kiss before I made my way back to my seat. Harriet, Mary V., and Dianne were waiting for me. There were lots of squeals, hugs, and tears, as you could imagine! Barry said of my performance, "Linda was definitely not in a coma. She was real calm up here." When Barry finished signing my video, he said, "You did great, darlin', great!" I was on cloud nine!!

Well, I've got the video tape beside me and if it is still here when I wake up in the morning, then I'll know this wasn't all a dream. I'll let you know tomorrow. Good night, Diary.

Love,
Linda

"*I grew up in Utah* and I was discriminated against because I didn't belong to the popular religion and many times felt like an outcast," described Laura Conners. During her Grade School and Junior High years, Laura racked up countless music lessons. In High School she eagerly volunteered for stage crew duties for the plays and productions that ran. Laura was always a little "different" and it was obvious amongst her peers. "Everyone I knew got married right out of High School or shortly thereafter." But, not Laura. Instead of taking the familiar path of marriage, Laura decided to go on to college.

While attending the University of Utah in 1974, Laura heard "Mandy" play on her radio. There was something about the song and the singer that made her want to hear more of him. During this same time, Laura had a special someone, a serviceman, away in Germany. One day, Laura received a "Dear Jane" letter from her beloved. The masterfully crafted lyrics that Laura kept hearing again and again made "Mandy" a song that she deeply connected with. That song described her desires so closely, so completely. Painfully, Laura resolved that she would never allow herself to love again.

But life went on, and Laura did find love. She married and settled into a new life. Along the way, she continued to follow Barry Manilow's career until around 1984 when Barry seemed to have faded from public view. Laura figured that was as good a time as any to absorb herself in her family and business. She saturated herself with everybody's needs and dreams but her own. "I lost sight of things that were a part of me because I thought they were not practical," Laura described. "I thought, 'Who needs The Arts?'"

But to the unsuspecting Laura, one single night and one spectacular Barry Manilow concert would soon change her life forever. The year was 1993 and Laura's husband treated her to her very first Manilow concert. Just sitting in the theatre that evening, Laura's attitude about The Arts, music and performance rapidly started to change. There was a transformation, a metamorphosis about to take place. While browsing through the tour book Laura purchased at the concert, she noticed the information printed about his International Fan Club. "It took me a while to overcome my insecurities about joining a fan club," said Laura. "I thought that a married woman shouldn't join. That was for teenagers or star crossed groupies, people who were not serious about life. Those people were fantasy chasers, unrealistic dreamers. Besides, what would my husband and other people think of me?"

After toying with the idea, Laura decided to give it a go. Twenty years had passed and Laura was going to start living life again. "I had to find out more about Barry and his life. Who cared what others thought," Laura said. "I was going to do this for me!"

Laura Conners
aka CSWY girl for a night.
Her unforgettable experience is
captured on film.

(Photo by Darlene Schwartz.)

You know what else she did for herself? She became a Can't Smile girl. Laura wanted it to happen and she made herself available to be chosen. That is certainly a huge leap from where she was not so many years ago.

Laura's being chosen to sing with Barry was not just an event, it was an adventure. Laura began driving her friends and family half crazy as she started thinking about the sign she would make to draw attention to herself at the concerts. Then, she got a copy of her best Barry Buddy's video who was a Can't Smile girl, and she began to study it. She watched it over and over just to make sure she had the routine down pat. Then, Laura went coast to coast on her quest. Her first stop from her California home was Las Vegas. With a 55" kite in tow, she headed to the airport. When checking her baggage she was always asked what was in the long box. When she told them a kite, she received many strange looks. Laura wrestled with the kite box and three pieces of luggage all the way to the JFK airport. From there, she and Barry Buddy, Darlene, rented a car and drove to a Connecticut concert with the kite taking up the front and back seat. "It's these 'problems' that make touring so much fun," said Laura.

When the 1997 Radio City Music Hall concert dates arrived, Laura was ready. She had been hauling the kite around from state to state and by this time, she had it down to a science. But, when she got to the RCMH show, security began giving her a hassle over the kite. After the first couple of nights, security left her alone and Laura was able to breathe a sigh of relief. Unfortunately, the New York run didn't turn out to be her lucky spot. Laura was beginning to doubt the power of her kite. She knew Barry had to have seen it. A person would have to be visually impaired not to see it.

In spite of Laura's frustration, she had a dream that she was on stage with Barry and she was wearing a yellow dress with her blue flowered scarf. This gave her the encouragement she needed to forge ahead to Chicago. Once again, she was plagued with concern over her sign by Rosemont security. She was told that she would be thrown out of the show if she didn't put it away. Laura explained that the sign was only for the CSWY portion of the show. So, the security personnel told her she could hold her sign up for 15 seconds and he would be timing her.

The second night at Rosemont, Laura donned her yellow dress with her kite pin that Darlene had given her for good luck. During intermission, Laura had a decision to make. Either stand in line for the bathroom or put her 52" kite together. She opted for the ladies room first, eating away 20 minutes of the intermission. Laura chose not to put her kite together for this CSWY segment.

Barry came back out on stage and began his second half of the show in the usual way, singing "Can't Smile Without You," scanning the audience for his next "victim." Laura had a gut feeling that she was going to be chosen. She took her scarf and waved it in the air. Laura, in the third seat from the aisle, was then selected as the next CSWY gal. All of Laura's anticipation and preparation paid off, even without that kite!

Laura recalled, "Barry has the most fantastic eyes and face! I wanted to make sure that his face and eyes were burned into my memory because this moment would have to last me a lifetime. He smelled so good and it was so comforting being in his arms. His aura wrapped around me and it was as though only he and I were there."

Laura always thought that she'd suffer extreme stage fright when her big moment arrived, but, that was the furthest thing from her mind. She even stole a glance into the audience. She wanted to see what Barry saw. "I found that he sees hardly anything, only blackness," described Laura. "But boy, can he hear the noise!"

Laura has her prized video of her CSWY duet to always remind her of her moments with Barry. She watches her video and instantly, she is there once again. During the concerts immediately following her CSWY moment, she had a hard time remembering not to stand up in anticipation to be selected. She has since gotten that under control.

"I hope everyone who wants to sing with Barry has the opportunity. He is truly a gentle man and a gentleman," Laura described. "Thank you, Barry for taking such good care of me on stage. I am so grateful that you are extremely musical and talented."

If Laura ever had to experience what Bill Murray did in "Groundhog Day," Laura would want that one day to be May 31, 1997, the day she became Barry's "Can't Smile Without You" girl.

*"I'm still a wannabe* 'Can't Smile' girl," explained Janelle Graves. Janelle lives in a suburb of Portland, Oregon. Janelle, along with her Barry

friend whom she met via the Internet, drove to one of Barry's concerts in Seattle in 1997. With many Manilow tapes to keep them company, Janelle and her friend managed to sing their way from Oregon to Washington State, never missing a beat. Actually, Janelle was really practicing up for her "Can't Smile" debut that she would be so desperately trying to expedite that evening.

Janelle experienced a couple of "firsts" during the concert in Seattle. That concert would be the first time she would be seated close enough to the stage to see Barry's beautiful blue eyes without the aid of binoculars and it would also be the first time she would make a sign for the "Can't Smile" portion of Barry's show.

As predicted, the "Can't Smile" segment began and Janelle hoisted her sign high in the air, hoping Barry's attention would be drawn to it. The phrase Janelle chose to put on her sign might lead one to believe that she had the utmost confidence that she would be assured of that coveted spot standing right next to Barry on stage. Janelle's sign read, "You Can't Sing Without Me, Barry." Barry chose one of her friends instead.

*Sandy Lapiska has seen* Barry in concert over 85 times. From her first Barry concert in 1977, she knew her first show wouldn't be her last. Then, when the "Can't Smile" segment took shape, she was determined not to give up trying to become a "Can't Smile Without You" girl until her mission was accomplished. Sandy stayed true to her word and after her 66th show, Sandy was initiated into this prestigious and much sought-after club.

The weekend prior to Thanksgiving, 1995, Sandy attended two concerts in Orlando, Florida, at the Bob Carr Performing Arts Theatre. A veteran sign-maker for the "Can't Smile" song, Sandy chose a holiday theme for the sign she would take to the two shows. With some help from her friend Cheryl, they came up with a clever idea. (Cheryl was a good one to ask about things of this nature since she was chosen to sing with Barry in May while in Las Vegas.) They agreed that a turkey would grace Sandy's sign. Not just any turkey would do. So, they searched high and low and came across a crepe paper turkey centerpiece that would be just perfect. As if the crepe paper turkey wasn't enough, Sandy's caption for the sign, "DON'T BE A TURKEY, PICK ME!" put the finishing touch on this sign

Perhaps the idea for the sign was more of a revelation? The morning of the concert, Sandy said she went to church and "asked the Lord for one special favor." You guessed it. Sandy had prayed and she was prepared. Sandy should have known she was touched by an Angel as things began falling in line for her as the evening of the concert rolled around. First, as Sandy and her friends drove into the parking area of the Theatre, they circled around to finally land in the parking spot behind Barry's vehicle. Another sign of her impending meeting with Barry was when Sandy turned to her friend and said, "I'm going to get glitter all over Barry tonight." No, she wasn't going to rush the stage in sheer vigilante style with a bucket of sparkles, she was wearing a shirt that had white glitter on it. Then, to top it all off, when the time came for Barry to perform "Can't Smile Without You," Sandy automatically reached for her bird and popped Tic-Tacs in her mouth.

Sure enough, the sign caught his attention and Sandy's most wished-for opportunity of a lifetime came true. Barry pointed to her sign, summoned her to the stage and before she knew it, Sandy was telling Barry how good he felt. She insists she wasn't nervous. With a microphone in one of Sandy's hands and Barry's hand in her other hand, they strolled across the stage singing. The time flew and then Sandy graciously accepted her hug and kiss from Barry.

At intermission, Sandy and her girlfriends hurried to the lobby pay phones so Sandy could phone home and share the good news with her family. The phones were all in use but finally, one became available and Sandy dialed only to get the answering machine on the other end. She had to share her excitement with somebody, so, she screamed into the phone, "Barry picked me for Can't Smile!" When Sandy returned home that evening, she was elated to find that her message had got through as her father stood in her driveway singing "Can't Smile Without You." At that moment, Sandy was confident that her father would NEVER again tease her about her love for Barry. Her father was quite eager to tell anyone who would listen that his daughter got to sing with Barry Manilow.

As Sandy looks back on that glorious evening, she regrets that she didn't think to thank Barry for selecting her to sing with him. If she had it to do all over again, Sandy said she'd like to whisper in Barry's ear, "Thank you for picking me to sing with you." For Sandy, she'd gladly trade "15 minutes of fame" for "five magic minutes" with Barry again, any day!

*Susanne Haggberg has tried* practically everything besides standing on her head to get the attention of Barry Manilow during the ever popular "Can't Smile Without You" segments. Since the beginning of Barry's pop career Susanne has liked his music, but, it was when she heard the VSM (AKA: Very Strange Medley) that she clearly recalls being the turning point from "casual listener" to "serious fan."

Let us take a moment to review some of the things Susanne has attempted in her quest to sing with Barry. Susanne has certainly dressed for the occasion by choosing to wear shiny, reflective clothing for certain shows. That would surely grab Barry's attention, right? At another concert, Susanne sported her then newly-acquired "Harmony" T-shirt. She thought she might strike a chord with Barry knowing his passion for this moving musical he and collaborator Bruce Sussman created. Well, that didn't work either.

So, if the clothing didn't seem to do the trick, maybe some pulsating lights and lavish signs might capture Barry's attention. Although Susanne can't remember exactly each sign she has made in the past, one of the most recent signs she has toted to Barry's concerts read, "I'd Really Love To Sing With You Tonight," to commemorate Barry's tour which featured his super successful, *Summer of '78* CD. She had that phrase lettered on a colossal, fluorescent board with big, shiny bows attached to it. That did not work. Not only has Susanne tried catching Barry's eye with Christmas lights, she has even gone one step further by firing up a strobe light on one occasion. Those didn't work either.

The answer to that question is as individual as each person and the formula Barry uses to select the lucky gals is left for each hopeful "Can't Smile" candidate to ponder. In the meantime, until Susanne is selected to sing with

Barry, she will have to reinvent her strategies and most of all, she'll have to be patient. To swap possible "Can't Smile" tactics or to divulge secrets that have worked for you "Can't Smile" gals out there, visit Susanne's Manilow-dedicated webpage at http://members.aol.com/manilow2 and be sure to drop her a note.

## A Brave Night
### By Margaret Kelly

*Barry asked for a* "brave lady" to sing with him at the Mirage in Las Vegas on August 29, 1995, so I raised my hand. I was in the American West for the first time in my life with my very first fan-friend I ever had, Candee, sitting nearby. Years ago, Candee had made me promise her that if I ever got picked as a "Can't Smile" girl, she would be the first person I'd call, after my Mother, of course.

After hearing Barry say that he wanted to pick someone who really wanted to sing with him, I stood on my chair so I would have a better chance of being seen. I was surprisingly calm as I waited for Barry to come over to my side of the stage as he scanned the audience. This was the last of a six-show run and it was the end of a very trying summer for me due to a variety of medical tests I had endured. So, this night, I was almost literally numb from exhaustion.

As Barry approached my side of the stage, a taller girl stood up on a chair directly in front of me. I too, was standing on my chair so because of my short stature, I leaned into the isle to be better seen by Barry. To my amazement, Barry saw me and called out, "You in the green!" I was wearing a green blouse.

I jumped off my chair and flew down a small flight of steps, maneuvering around people milling in the aisle and grabbed the then house manager, Victor's one hand with both of mine. He handed me up the stairs leading to the stage and to Barry, who was saying something about not stumbling on the edge of the stage. So, naturally, the toe of my shoe caught the lip of the stage. Instinctively, I grabbed Barry's arm with both hands in fear that I would fall onto the stage.

Barry has once said that he sings to Exit lights. That is no lie. As he led me to the piano, I scanned the audience looking for my friends. Because of the two large Super Trooper spotlights aimed right at us, it was impossible to make out any faces. The stream of lights made it seem as if Barry and I were enclosed in an oval of soft white curtains. I couldn't see or hear anyone! I thought, "this gives me more time to concentrate on Barry's face." He appeared to be even thinner in the face than I recalled from meeting him at signings. He had only a little sweat on his temples.

I was also thinking about how comfortable I was with Barry. He was so hospitable that I felt as if I were a guest in his living room. In spite of my experience in community theatre and on stage, I was well aware that this was much bigger than my past experiences: I was on the stage of the Barry Manilow Show and this was a very famous showroom - the Mirage!

Barry asked my occupation and I answered, "Insurance Investigator for the State of New York." Barry seemed impressed and said, "Wow, that sounds serious!" With my arm around his waist, I began to gently rub his back. Because I was his guest, I decided to keep my hand above his belt and not go any lower - I didn't want him to boot me off the stage for being unladylike. Then he said, "You don't look serious." Not knowing how to

respond to this comment, I opted to enjoy the feeling of his jacket fabric instead.

"Do you know the words to 'Can't Smile,'" Barry asked? After attending 51 concerts, I was able to give him a definite, "Yes!" As he dropped my hand on the piano to get the microphone I'd be using, I realized the top of the piano was covered with felt. Maybe that is why I've seen him pick lint off the top of the piano in various concerts.

I held the microphone in my left hand and held on to Barry's hand with my right and we began to sing. We were at arm's length from each other; I wanted to be closer. I gently tugged his hand to try to put it around my waist. I'm so short that his hand cupped my left shoulder instead! I felt the side of my face on his chest and heard him chuckle. I felt so calm and safe with Barry, I wished I could stay against his chest forever.

By nature, I am not an emotional person, but at one point, he gave me such a sexy look with his eyes, I had to quickly break eye contact or I feared I would faint. Barry softly cued me with "let's dance," and we danced as I glanced at his feet to make sure I matched him step for step. He gripped my hand tighter and my hand disappeared in his long, strong fingers. I could have danced all night.

Barry hopped onto the piano and took his famous, "Can't Smile" seated position. He nestled me between his legs as they hung over the edge. I felt somewhat uneasy about this, then I noticed his hand on my hair, and that calm, secure feeling came rushing back to me.

Barry jumped down from the piano and I buried my head in his chest. My moments with Barry were coming to an end so I concentrated on what I really wanted; a really good hug. And what a hug Barry gives! I desperately tried to cover his whole back with my tiny hands. He held me so firmly, yet gently, that I had the sensation of being pulled into his chest and against his heart. This hug was the first one I had received in a very long time. I wanted to live on that hug forever.

At the edge of the stage I received my kiss from Barry. I've always been considered a bad kisser, so I made sure I got Barry right on the lips! I was determined to get one more hug, so I reached up as high as I could and flung my left arm around Barry's neck. He stooped a bit and let me hug him one last time. He handed me back to Victor and I returned to my seat for the rest of the show.

After the show, Candee ran up to me, screaming for joy, and before she could speak, I said, "Candee, I just want to tell you, Barry picked me for 'Can't Smile!'"

*In May, 1997, Mary* Boicken of Homewood, Illinois, attended her first Barry Manilow concert. She certainly remembers hearing "Mandy" back in the 70s and being struck by the beautiful music. But, on December 21, 1997, Mary received a beautiful Christmas surprise.

Mary's concert-buddy roommates kept teasing and tormenting Mary for taking so long to get ready for the concert that night. Mary was taking extra special precaution in her appearance as she told her pals, "I want to look my best in case I get picked to sing on stage with Barry." The concert was at the MGM Grand Garden Arena in Las Vegas, so, Mary wanted to wear something sort of glitzy in honor of the famed city she was visiting. Why not! Barry Manilow in Las Vegas. Who could ask for more?

After attending only two Manilow concerts, Mary caught on rather quickly to the pomp and circumstance that takes place among those fans who want to be chosen to sing "Can't Smile Without You" with Barry. Being a keen observer, Mary knew she had the outfit in the bag. She was just hoping the sign she had made would aid in her mission to be chosen. Borrowing a song title from Barry's *Showstoppers* CD, Mary constructed her sign of hot pink by penning "REAL LIVE GIRL" in huge black letters.

When the "Can't Smile" segment arrived, Mary had a feeling, a very good feeling. The signs began popping up throughout the venue, including Mary's hot pink sign. Barry walked out on stage and began the ritual. According to Mary, it must have been her sign that Barry noticed first, but, once the house lights were turned up so Barry could survey the crowd, Mary's lucky feeling became much stronger. "I was wearing a black jacket with a lot of spangles on it," Mary said. "He didn't see my outfit until they turned the house lights on and he saw me and my sign first thing. I guess I looked very Las Vegas." And that was a good thing for Mary.

"I could tell right away he was going to pick me, but, he still went through the whole thing of looking over the crowd. I could tell I was going to be picked because he kept flashing his eyes to me the whole time, no matter where he was on the stage," Mary noticed. She was right.

"Saying getting picked was a thrill is a gross understatement," said Mary. "My feet never touched the ground the whole time. He held me so tight to him. I really didn't want to sing, I just wanted him to keep holding me! When the song was over and we kissed good bye, I felt like Cinderella leaving the ball too soon."

Mary commented how the five minutes with Barry on stage went by so fast. "Thank goodness we get a video tape of the experience afterwards. I could barely remember being up there with him, but, this five minutes in 'Heaven' will last me for a lifetime, and then some."

Was it just coincidence that Mary was chosen to sing with Barry while attending only her third concert? One can't be sure, but, check this out. Mary became interested in Barry's music three years after getting through the death of her parents. Her birthday was exactly three months prior to the night she got chosen to sing with Barry. Her seat for the concert was located on the floor in section three. And, while in Las Vegas, she stayed at the MGM on the 13th floor of the hotel. "Three has become my new lucky number," beamed Mary.

*On November 28, 1988*, it was raining outside but the weather couldn't dampen the spirits of the Exeter Friends Barry Manilow Fan Club of Exeter, England. One by one, they boarded a bus that would take them to Bournemouth for a Barry Manilow concert. Throughout their journey, the conversation was Barry, Barry, and more Barry.

They arrived in Bournemouth early so they could get a little shopping in and partake in a leisurely meal before they headed to the BIC for the show. Once there, they perused the souvenir stand and of course, visited the ladies room to freshen up their makeup. Along with the usual powder, lipstick and blush, Lauraine Dobson had packed her toothbrush with her cosmetics. As her fellow club members teased Lauraine, she proceeded to brush her teeth.

Lauraine found her seat, located 21 rows back from the stage. Was she ever glad she brought her binoculars! The music began and there stood Barry. Lauraine was breathless. Song followed song and before long the notes of "Can't Smile Without You" began to ring out. Lauraine and her pals jumped up and down as Barry walked toward the front of the stage. He looked Lauraine's direction and pointed saying, "Yes, you with the binoculars."

"When I got to the stage," Lauraine recalled, "I was lost in his deep blue eyes." Barry began their conversation asking Lauraine a few questions about herself; her name, where she lived, and what her job was. Then, he asked a most unusual question that would take most by surprise; he asked her if she was married. Without batting an eye, Lauraine responded, "No, not tonight!" He offered her the microphone in which she would be using and as she reached out to take it, her hands began to shake. A normal response. She was, after all, in the presence of Barry Manilow and on a stage in front of thousands.

After singing, strolling, hugging and kissing, Lauraine had to let him go and return to her seat. On her way there, Barry called out her name so she went back to the stage and he presented her with an autographed video of their duet. He signed, "With love and thanks, Barry Manilow: November 28, 1988."

The rest of the concert was a bit of a blur for Lauraine as she found it extremely hard to concentrate. When intermission arrived, Lauraine was mobbed by fans who wanted to touch her face because Barry had touched it. They asked question after question in attempt to absorb even a smidgen of what Lauraine had just experienced. Eventually Lauraine reached a telephone. She called her husband to tell him that Barry had chosen her to sing with him. Her husband didn't believe her at first, but, she finally managed to convince him.

Over the next few days, Lauraine became somewhat of a celebrity in her hometown, being interviewed by local radio stations and newspapers. Several people even recognized her stopping her on the street to inquire about her moments with Barry Manilow. All the time, she kept telling them about the depth of his beautiful blue eyes.

Years and many concerts have passed since Lauraine's personal moment with Barry, but, one thing remains the same. As Lauraine prepares to attend Barry's concerts, she meticulously packs her purse with plenty of cosmetics for a quick touch-up and she never leaves the house until she is sure her toothbrush is in there too.

*"If you are looking* for a quick and extravagant 'Can't Smile Without You' story, you may want to look elsewhere," Lisa Pare wrote about her treasured moments with Barry Manilow on June 18, 1997. Lisa got her opportunity to share the stage with Barry at her very first concert. She had listened to his music for over 23 years, but had never had the pleasure of seeing him live. So, how did she manage to get chosen to sing with Barry at her first concert? "You'll have to take that one up with God," explained Lisa, "I had nothing to do with it."

Although Lisa has loved Barry and his music for 23-plus years, she had to put him on the back-burner, so to speak, while a "cyclone hit the rest of my life," Lisa said. Lisa has loved music her entire life and her dream was to, one day, become a singer in a band. Unfortunately, her parents didn't have the same dreams for Lisa's future so they discouraged her from pursuing her music career. But somebody else was there to cheer Lisa on. It was

Barry Manilow. Lisa vividly remembers singing along with Barry's albums as a young girl growing up. Her time spent with Barry was special. Through his lyrics and melodies, he inspired Lisa to keep making music even when everyone else scoffed her.

Lisa wrote many songs and poems, but not necessarily out of sheer creativity. In actuality, she penned these pieces to get her through what she refers to as her "emotional black-out." This was during a period of years when Lisa got married, had a beautiful son, almost died, got separated, and then got divorced. This may sound "neat" and "effortless" on paper, but in reality, Lisa's world was falling apart. Barry's music was the only constant in Lisa's life as she rode choppy, nauseating waves of despair. Then, as if all this wasn't enough of a load for Lisa to bear, she discovered that she had breast cancer. Coupled with that, severe depression practically suffocated her will to live.

When Lisa made the decision to see Barry in concert after all of those years of leaning on his therapeutic music, she could hardly believe it was going to finally happen. She and her 13 year old son were going to make the 8 hour trip by car from their home in California to Phoenix, Arizona, to meet up with the many friends Lisa had made on the Internet. Together, they would form a bond so strong, so undeniable, that they knew it could only be one man who would have ever brought them together in this way. They were going to celebrate that in their time together and at the concert they would soon attend.

Lisa was not going to the concert empty-handed. She had heard all about the signs hopeful CSWY gals make, so, she was definitely going to try her hand at the sign-making extravaganza too. Her sign, "I NEED YOU...MANILOW ME!" was self-reflective. She did need Barry and she certainly wanted to be "Manilowed." "I never totally believed I had a real chance of getting picked, but when you have breast cancer, you aim high" Lisa explained. Ready to burst into little pieces from excitement, she and her son entered the venue, took their seats and enjoyed the show. When the CSWY segment began, Lisa grabbed her sign and held it high in the air. She didn't jump up and down or yell and scream. That is not her style. She just stood there and smiled, sang and PRAYED! The next thing she knew, her son was telling her, "Mom, you got picked, GO!" Then, he said it again! Lisa was stunned.

With her heart pounding, she ran to the stage with Barry standing there waiting to take her hand. "All I could do was look into those baby blues and try to forget there were 3,000 people in front of me even though I could hear their cheers of support," remembered Lisa. "Barry was so wonderful to me. It was almost like he knew that my life had been somewhat hellish and he was about to make it all better. I was shaking like a leaf but I totally trusted him." Then, it began. Lisa's magic moment. Barry and Lisa chatted and laughed, sang and danced, hugged and kissed….and hugged and kissed! Lisa wasn't going to let this once-in-a-lifetime-moment pass her by without making the most of it!

"My dream was to hug Barry and show him how much I loved him and his music and for saving my life with his love and support," Lisa said. "I have been able to live my musical dream through him and for a few wonderful moments, he even let me share his passion with him on stage. Thank you God for sparing my life and allowing my dream with Barry to come true. I am forever grateful."

There is no shortage of smiles as Robbie Steed and Barry sang together at the Reunion Arena in Dallas, Texas.

Barry and CSWY girl, Laura Mingo, make
music together.

# Chapter Five

# Read 'em
# And Weep

Life sometimes has its way of throwing curveballs every now and again. How we react to these bumps and turns is completely up to us. We can wallow in self-pity and generally feel sorry for ourselves, or, we can pick ourselves up, dust ourselves off and look at ways of extracting the positive out of what can sometimes seem to be insurmountable odds. Sometimes, it seems easier to get down on ourselves, convincing ourselves that things will never get better. The other path, the path to recovery, personal victory and success, many times, takes a little work. It takes perseverance, positive thinking and action. Though the journey toward this victory can be long and difficult, the personal satisfaction you will receive for your endurance is highly rewarding and empowering.

For those Barry Manilow fans who have shared their stories (some for the first time ever), life's knocks certainly camped on their doorsteps, but, only for a short time. Barry's songs have pulled fans through divorce, death of loved ones, abuse, illness, and depression because of the powerful, reflective, and honest lyrics. In many cases, it is through those poignant words of a Manilow tune that some fans attribute much of their ability to cope with their circumstances. Through the lyrics, they have learned that they are not alone in their trials, they will rise above the challenges and in the end, they will come out on top. The melodies of a Manilow tune intricately tap into their hearts and souls, fastening a stronghold that never lets go and never lets you forget.

The following stories reveal that with love and hope, nothing is impossible. May these stories inspire us to reach within ourselves and to reach to others for the spark that ignites the flame of change, belief, and survival.

*Young, energetic, and creative* Nancy Rosebrugh of Mission Viejo, California, is a jewelry designer and has recently started her own business. When you think of a person who starts a business, you probably envision that person being self confident, a progressive thinker, and in general, a person who possesses a persevering personality which allows nothing to get them down. Just a few years ago, Nancy wouldn't have fit into any of those categories. But after reading Barry Manilow's autobiography, *Sweet Life: Adventures On The Way To Paradise,* Nancy changed her doubting and discouraged ways. In Nancy's words, "It (the book) gave me encouragement to go out and try to do something that I enjoyed doing for a living."

The book also gave her courage to take a risk and take a chance. This is a brave undertaking for someone who once thought of taking her own life. The same year that Barry lost his mother, Nancy's mother died very slowly and very painfully from a rare form of liver disease. Six months after her Mother's passing, her Father had quadruple bypass surgery for a condition worsened by the stress of dealing with the loss of his wife. Two months later, Nancy chipped a bone in her knee and broke her femur in half in a freak accident. She spent a week in the hospital and the next three months in a hospital bed at home. It took a wheelchair for Nancy to perform even the most simple of tasks around her home. That same month, her beloved cocker spaniel, Buffy, died after having surgery. To top it all off, Nancy's boyfriend broke up with her and moved to Europe with a new girlfriend. "My life was shattered," Nancy recalled. "I considered suicide but then thought it would just be more heartache for my family who had stood by me through all of this."

But Nancy's world was about to be rocked one more time, this time for the better. That Christmas, Nancy received Barry's box set, *The Complete Collection And Then Some*, for a gift. "That box set was my lifeline in this troubled storm. It brought out all the feelings that I had bottled up inside; all the sadness, frustration, anxiety, etc." Nancy said. Nancy listened to every word of every song and miraculously, nearly every song sounded like it was meant for her alone. Many of the songs helped her from being afraid of the future and provided her with an unexplainable comfort.

"By listening to this music," said Nancy, "I literally started to heal. The wounds deep inside were closing. Barry put back the song in my heart and I wanted to sing again." Singing was a hobby of Nancy's and through all of her troubles, she had lost even this desire. Nancy began to be happy again and felt as if she was finally able to go on with her life.

To help heal her inner wounds, those emotional scars that are sometimes the hardest ones to treat, Nancy wanted to share her experiences with the man who helped her through the darkest period of her life. She wrote Barry Manilow a 25 page letter telling him of her tragedies, her triumphs and that he occupied a very special place in her heart. Even though Barry wasn't there physically, Nancy drew from the passion in his voice, the power of the lyrics and the peace of the melodies.

These days you can find Nancy volunteering for various charities through the Barry Manilow Fan Clubs she is involved with as well as pursuing her hectic but exciting new career as a jewelry designer and entrepreneur. And although these two words may seem simple, Nancy, once again wanted to share her deep and heartfelt appreciation by saying, "Thanks, Barry!"

"*My father died very* suddenly at age 57 in 1992. I had just started the job where I am now four days before he died, was 2,000 miles away in Alabama (he lived in California) and got the phone call from the hospital after he had been dead for about two hours. As you can imagine, with no warning and no chance to say 'good bye' it understandably knocked the wind out of my sails for quite some time. I considered my dad not only my 'dad' but also one of my best friends," recalled Lyn Arnold.

As the months passed, Lyn's friends and family mentioned to her that they missed the "old" Lyn, the Lyn who used to laugh a great deal, found humor in almost everything, and who cared so passionately about the things in life that mattered to her. She just couldn't seem to find real joy in anything through her grief.

The bright light was soon to shine at the end of her long tunnel of despair. Barry was scheduled to perform in Birmingham, Alabama, on his *Greatest Hits* tour in July, 1993. Ironically, this was almost exactly one year since her father's death. Uncharacteristically, Lyn didn't even attempt to get tickets. As a birthday present to Lyn, a friend of hers purchased tickets for them both. Lyn was looking forward to going, but, not as she usually would have.

The night arrived and Lyn and her friend settled in for Barry's performance. "I can honestly say that hearing his beautiful voice that I love so much and seeing his energy on stage once again was honestly and truly the first time in almost a year I had been glad I was alive," explained Lyn. "As my tears were flowing when he sang 'I Am Your Child' and 'Could It Be Magic,' I was reminded of how I have always thought his voice is like 'heaven on earth' and that was something to be joyful about."

"I don't think I could ever fully describe the effect he had on me that night," recalled Lyn. "It was like coming out of a very long and very bad dream. Nothing had 'jump started' me for the whole year like hearing him sing live did. My personal gratitude to Barry for that will last until I die."

Lyn's friends and family are also very thankful to have their Lyn back. "I have kidded with my friends through the years that although I don't attend church with regularity anymore, I do belong to the Church of Barry, and that is enough!" proclaimed Lyn.

Scenes from a Barry Manilow concert.

*Barbara Lovejoy's mother was* diagnosed with cancer in 1984. Two and one-half years later, Barbara's mother was gone. In order to take care of her mom in her final months, Barbara gave up Barry, but not completely. She still listened to his music, but, she withdrew from the concert-going scene. While Barbara packed her bags and moved to Florida to be with her mom, she packed away all of her Manilow mementos and placed them in storage. Barbara kept telling herself, "Now that mom's gone, I have to become a more responsible person and I'm getting too old to be chasing around after Barry."

Several years passed and Barbara became that responsible person she kept telling herself she should be. She had a great job, a beautiful home and all the responsibilities that come along with being responsible. Somewhere in all of her "success," she lacked fun, plain and simple. Barbara didn't allow herself this luxury, after all, things were going great for her, on the surface. Then, when she least expected it, the bottom fell out of her perfect life. The hospital where she worked began laying off employees, including Barbara. Within a matter of time, Barbara lost her home and the bills began to mount. Barbara was certain there was no way out of her predicament.

One night while taking a shower, Barbara's emotions overcame her and she began sobbing. She started to tell God how tired she was and that she couldn't take any more. She didn't know how she was going to face one more disappointment, one more job rejection, and one more bill that she couldn't pay. God was listening.

A voice started speaking to her inside her head. It said, "Don't give up Barb. You can give in, you can give out, but, you don't give up." She just knew these words sounded familiar to her. Where had she heard them before? Barbara began telling herself, "Don't give up, don't give up." The very next day, her life took a turn for the better. A few days later, Barbara decided to watch Barry's *Live on Broadway* video. Out of the mouth of Manilow came those prophetic words she had heard just days before. "It was like a lightning bolt had struck me. I started questioning why I wasn't having any fun in my life and I asked myself when I had the most fun" said Barbara. It took her all of three seconds to answer herself: when she followed Barry Manilow.

Without hesitation, she retrieved all of her Manilow items from storage. She poured through each item as she cried and laughed and relived every precious memory. "I never realized how much joy Barry had given me until then. I think my mother would approve knowing how much Barry meant to me before she became sick," Barbara reflected.

Since then, Barbara moved to Murfreesboro, Tennessee, landed a wonderful job and found a great place to live. She made new friends and she is much closer to other members of her family who live in Memphis. By bringing Barry's career back into her life, Barbara has also been able to finish another chapter in her life; she has found closure in her mom's passing. "I found the courage to say good-bye to my mom after 11 years," Barbara said.

On Barbara's refrigerator is a small piece of paper that reads:

> "You can give in..
>  You can give out..
>  But, you don't give up!"
>  —Barry Manilow

Manilow fans at the Copa in New York City. From left to right, Darlene Schwartz, the author, Mandy Strunk, Ann Underwood, and Betty Sadowski.

*Mary Alberstadt fondly remembers* the many times in her life when Barry Manilow's music has embraced and comforted her. From the early days, when "Mandy" hit the charts to today, Mary can give several accounts of times that Barry's music has made a difference in her life.

Mary was 11 years old when she first heard "Mandy" on the car radio as she was going home from school. Even then, she recognized the power of Barry's music. What she didn't realize, was that Barry Manilow's music would, to this day, continue to speak to her as plainly as it did all those years ago.

In 1981, Mary was a freshman in college and had plans to see Barry in concert in Buffalo, New York. On the same night as the concert, Mary's school would be hosting a dance and much to Mary's delight, she was asked to this dance by a pre-med student she has absolutely crazy about. Mary was faced with a huge decision. Should she go on this first date with the budding doctor or should she turn him down to attend the Manilow show? After vacillating over her choices, Mary did the only thing a true Manilow fan would do in that situation...she went to see Barry.

On the 1 1/2 hour trip to the concert that evening, Mary began to have second thoughts about her decision. "I kept saying to myself, 'Stupid! Stupid! You should have gone to the dance,'" said Mary. But the moment Barry walked out on stage, all the emotional battering went away. She knew she made the correct decision. "I never regretted my decision for another second," Mary explained. "He was magnificent, and my true dream guy."

When Mary returned to school Monday morning following the concert, she heard that her pre-med man had met someone else. This was a blessing in disguise for Mary because not only did Mr. Medicine marry this college sweetheart, just four years later, Mary met the man who soon became her wonderful husband. They even have a picture in their home from the concert Mary attended to signify how much that concert changed their lives.

Like most married couples, Mary and her husband have endured their share of ups and downs throughout their years together. The Alberstadts continue to persevere throughout every trial they are faced with.

In September of 1996, Mary's husband, who was stricken with multiple sclerosis three years earlier, suffered a devastating fall. This fall caused injury to his spinal cord and was followed by a frightening year of being in and out of hospitals and nursing homes. The Alberstadts faced many difficulties which included horrifying bouts of loneliness. Mary even began suffering from frequent, debilitating panic attacks. Their families are very loving and supportive, but, they were unable to be with Mary and her husband because they lived almost 1200 miles away from them.

During this time, there were periods when Mary's husband was in a hospital two hours away from their home. Mary had to continue to work so they could pay the mounting medical bills. But, everyday, Mary would make the two hour trip to the hospital and two hour trip home to be with her husband. Mary's car became her second home. All she had to keep her company were her little Yorkshire Terrier, Tigger, and Barry Manilow's music.

Barry's music filled those frightening voids for Mary and kept her going, hour by hour, day by day. Mary's husband knows just how important Barry's music was to her as Mary has often said that she wouldn't have been able to remain strong throughout the ordeal if it weren't for Barry Manilow. After a year of this excruciating routine, Mary's husband came home to stay.

In November, 1997, Barry played Sunrise, Florida, and Mary and her husband were able to attend the concert. This was no small task for them physically or emotionally. It was their first outing since her husband's accident. During the concert, Mary's husband would look over at her to see her crying. "It was tears of joy he saw that night as I had not experienced such happiness in such a long time," Mary said. "I was also thrilled to have my husband sitting next to me at the concert, when many told us it would be impossible for him to do such things ever again. Barry had helped me come full circle."

Mary said that her husband is still not where he was before the accident, but, he continues physical therapy and is very determined. On one occasion, this determination resulted in a three mile walk to visit Barry's star on the Hollywood Walk of Fame. This may not sound like much of a feat, but, Mary was the one walking as she pushed her husband along in a wheelchair.

Several years ago, Mary and her husband swayed to "I Am Your Child" and "Could It Be Magic" at their wedding. In their life together, they continue to dance, although at times it is only by looking into each others' eyes. But, they know. Barry Manilow's music; timeless, powerful and riveting fills the Alberstadt home with joy and inspiration, even now.

Some other members of the Fan-family, (from left to right)
Stella Capp, Jim Muldoon, and Linda Horner.

*Sandra Dashwood was so moved* after she saw Barry Manilow in concert for her first time at the London Palladium, she immediately joined the UK BMIFC (Barry Manilow International Fan Club). That was 1990. For about a decade prior to her first concert, Sandra did as so many others have. She passively listened to Barry's music. But, it took her first live show to turn Sandra into the Manilow fan that she is today and to realize that she could learn a much greater lesson from the man, Barry Manilow.

Sandra not only listens to Barry's music, she listens to Barry's wisdom and words of advice that he frequently gives his audience when he performs. If you have attended a Barry Manilow concert, you have probably noticed his positive attitude and his inspiring messages of hope and perseverance. Sandra, too, hears these "pearls" and applies them to her own life.

During Barry's overseas concert appearances in 1998, Sandra was in the audience for 10 of his shows. She didn't go alone, as she has usually done in the past. This time, her friend Margaret traveled with her. But before they even set foot in the first concert venue, Sandra knew her journey following Barry from concert to concert would prove to be inspirational in many ways. The day before the start of the UK tour, Sandra was watching Barry's interview on ITV's *This Morning*. Glued to the TV set, she hung on Barry's every word, but, one sentence, in particular, hit her like a ton of bricks. To

Carol Trout gives Barry a hand.

paraphrase, Barry told his listening audience to look for the bigger reason why you are doing anything. Sandra was so encouraged by this statement that she decided while on her travels to the upcoming Manilow shows, she would jot down every inspirational comment that Barry proclaimed during the tour.

So, Sandra and Margaret readied themselves for lots of fun and loads of laughter; eager to make memories to the max. Sandra, of course, was on another quest all of her own. At the NEC in Birmingham, England, Sandra penned her first words of wisdom from Barry. She wrote: "What you do is not who you are—and who you are is just fine." She also wrote, "Have fun with your life. If you're doing something everyday which you don't like, don't do it. Find something you love to do and do that instead. If you're afraid, be afraid, and do it anyway. This is not a dress rehearsal."

Then, when the Cardiff show rolled around, Sandra was personally affected by some more wonderful words of wisdom. She mentioned how Barry explained the time, early in his career, when he "connected" with a bunch of strangers during a performance and his life was never quite the same thereafter. To Sandra, these words were almost prophetic to her. Sandra had recently began playing the guitar and studying music part-time. She was so moved by the concept of connecting with strangers that she has made it one of her life's goals to play her guitar so well, that she, too, will someday connect with a crowd of strangers through her music.

Then there was Wembley Arena. Toward the end of the show, Barry sang a powerful rendition of "Borrowed Time." The lyrics awakened Sandra. "This made me realize how every moment of our lives is very precious and each of the inspirational quotes which I had noted from Barry during the previous nights, suddenly took on a far deeper meaning," said Sandra.

Sandra and Margaret finished out the UK tour together, each show more moving and cherished than the last. Sandra absorbed the music, words, and essence of Barry Manilow. Sadly, it would be quite some time before she would see him perform live again. You might say that Barry Manilow has deeply motivated, encouraged, and even enlivened Sandra's approach to life and she would be the first to admit it. "The man and his music have transformed my life and given me a sense of purpose," said Sandra. And with this fervent rejuvenation, Sandra approaches each day ready to make the most of every hour. She continues to learn more about music and the guitar and she also puts her artistic abilities into action by drawing. Over the past few years, Sandra has put her pencil to paper and what flowed from her soul were captivating images of Barry. Sandra does not keep her talents to herself. On several occasions she has donated her original drawings to the UK BMIFC (Barry Manilow International Fan Club) to use as prizes in their charity functions. She also submits her work to a variety of Barry Manilow fan clubs so they may publish her drawings in their newsletters. She has also sent a few of her masterpieces to Barry.

Barry's inspiring words changed Sandra's perspective on her own life.

*Even before Debbie Waldron's* first Barry Manilow concert, she always had a soft spot in her heart for his music. This appreciation for Barry's style of music came because of the devotion and concern of a music teacher she had as a young girl in school. Debbie was a member of the school's choir and every Friday, the teacher played a different album, exposing the students to a variety of musical categories. On one particular Friday, the teacher went through the usual motions, placing the record on the player while she introduced the artist whom the students were about to hear. Special care was taken to point out particular techniques the artist used and why those details set that artist apart from other musicians.

As the teacher passed around the album jacket, the students read through the song list and looked at the photos and artwork used on the cover. The artist chosen for that day's lesson was Barry Manilow. When the album cover finally made it to Debbie, she looked it over taking a special fascination with the photo of Barry with his dog. "I thought, 'this guy is good but looks too sweet to make it,'" Debbie recalled. Barry's music stood out to Debbie as being different compared to the other albums the teacher had played for them. "The music, the lyrics were very different," Debbie remembered.

A few years passed and Debbie noticed one day that Barry Manilow would be performing in concert near her home. It didn't take her long to decide to attend the shows. Two nights in a row Debbie attended his concerts. They were the first and only concerts she had ever been to. "They were unreal, actually, like in a dream. The people, the noise level, the intense emotion from the crowd - very intense," Debbie said.

Then in the mid 80s, Debbie attended another of Barry's concerts. But over the years, many things in Debbie's life had changed dramatically. Health problems had gotten a foot-hold over Debbie and what was once an easy task to traipse out the front door of her home, hop in a car and drive anywhere, had become a thing of the past. Debbie's panic disorder had prevented her from doing many things, namely, driving a car.

The Scope, located in Norfolk, Virginia, was just a hop, skip and a jump from Debbie's hometown. But, for Debbie, this facility where Barry would be performing might as well have been in Washington State. Whenever Debbie drove, her panic attacks hit, causing a myriad of physical reactions. Among those were spastic colitis, reflux disease, and vomiting. But, Debbie was bound and determined not to let this opportunity to see Barry in concert pass her by, panic attack or no panic attack.

The only way she knew to get to the venue was by interstate. The eve of the concert, Debbie took a deep breath, climbed in her car and all by herself, drove via the interstate to the venue, parked her car, found her seat, took in the concert and reversed the procedure to get herself back home. Coupled with night blindness, this was a feat for Debbie. "It meant so much to me to drive so very far - to me it was far - and at night," said Debbie.

The next day, Debbie had to make a trip to her doctor for a shot; the only way to stop the excruciating pain of her colitis. It wasn't the first time she visited the doctor for a shot of this nature and according to Debbie, "the concert was well worth it. It was amazing!"

Today, Debbie works as a freelance graphic designer, digital artist and illustrator much of which is for non-profit organizations. She still battles with her panic disorder. Therefore, the majority of her work is done from her home in Virginia Beach, Virginia. Debbie is grateful for her experiences seeing Barry in concert and since she was so successful in getting to those, perhaps in the future, Debbie will make it to another show. She also desires to attend a Barry Manilow Convention. And with all of the love and support of her many Manilow fan-friends to help her, she'll do it. Visit Debbie's website at http://members.xoom.com/doodler for a peek at her creative designs.

*Isn't it ironic how* sometimes when you meet someone, the first impression you get about that person doesn't really excite you, but, given time that person becomes the best friend you could ever ask for? That is exactly what happened to Robbie Steed of Slidell, Lousiana. According to Robbie, Karen became her "best friend in the entire universe." Only hours after meeting, Robbie and Karen became closer than sisters in a relationship that continued for 11 years.

Robbie and Karen were Barry buddies, through and through. One day, just as true friends sometimes do, they had a slight falling out. But after Robbie called Karen to apologize and to explain to Karen what was going on in her life to make her so edgy, Karen seemed relieved to hear from Robbie. The girls were pals once again. Robbie and Karen could talk about anything under the sun and they shared the same fear of being hurt by others. Their closeness was based not only on their shared admiration for Barry but on their promise to each other to always be there for each other. And of course, they loved everything to do with Barry and enjoyed sharing prized possessions they would collect.

"Eventually, the miles between us and our personal lives took its toll on our friendship and I have not heard from her since December, 1994," said Robbie. Robbie's attempts to correspond with Karen were unfruitful. "My letters went unanswered, my cards were not responded to, so by the end of 1995, I stopped trying to contact her," Robbie said.

To make matters worse, Robbie has now lost track of Karen because of a move Robbie is sure Karen made from the address Robbie had. "I would give anything in this world to hear her voice again and to see her again," explained Robbie. "Part of me is praying that if this is mentioned in the book, maybe some sort of miracle could take place to put us back in touch. Not a day goes by that I don't realize there's a little something missing in my life."

Perhaps what Barry joined all those years ago could once again be brought together by the mere existence of this book. Karen, if you are reading this, Robbie wants you to know how much she misses you. Your presence in her life has forever altered her and the true friendship that you shared is desired once again. You may contact Robbie by e-mail at King_Of_Hearts_bmfc@yahoo.com.

*I had my first* lovely daughter, Melissa Ann, the day after my birthday in 1982. She was beautiful; dark black hair, olive skinned. After having her home only a week, she became ill and upon taking her to the doctor's office for what I thought would be a normal visit, turned into sheer terror.

The doctor discovered her heart was enlarged and they didn't know why until we arrived at Children's Hospital in Los Angeles, California. After examining our Melissa Ann, the Cardiologist told us she had a condition called Cardiomyopathy, in which the muscles in the left ventricle of her heart would thin out, deteriorate and the result would be death. They gave her six months to live.

I remember riding home that evening from the hospital thinking to myself, 'Is this a dream? Will I wake up and everything will be all right?' Well, it wasn't and as I arrived home, I found myself walking into our bedroom and seeing the empty bassinet beside my bed, breaking down once again.

Even though she was in and out of Children's Hospital the rest of 1982, Melissa proved a lot of doctors wrong. In October, 1982, I went to the hospital to bring her home as she took a turn for the better. I walked into the lobby area to obtain a pass to get Melissa when I saw about six or eight photographers standing around in the lobby. Nosy as I am, I asked the security person what they were there for. He told me that Barry Manilow was the Chairman that year for United Way and he'd be arriving any minute. I decided Melissa could wait just a few minutes and not less than five minutes later, a limousine pulled up and bigger than life, there was Barry Manilow.

A young female greeted Barry, shaking his hand. There were about 25 people there to welcome him. Barry was going to tour the hospital, leading up to a benefit concert at the Hollywood Bowl the next week or so. As Barry walked by, people shook his hand, saying 'hello.' I held out my hand too saying 'Hello, Barry' at which he grabbed my hand and said 'Hi, what's your name and why are you here?' After stumbling my words a little, I told him I was there to pick up my daughter, Melissa. He proceeded to ask me why she was there as we held hands walking to the elevator. I reached my floor, went to Melissa's room to dress her as my husband took care of the paperwork. I stepped into the hallway holding

Melissa looking for my husband and noticed some noise from down the hall. To my amazement, Barry and some others were walking out of the neonatal unit.

He saw me and threw up his hand and pointed to Melissa mouthing the words, 'is that her?' I shook my head 'yes.' He motioned for me to bring her to him. He started talking to her and asked if he could hold her. Melissa Ann was only six months old and very small for her age due to her heart problem. I took my hand, held his elbow that was under her and brought his arm around to hold her properly.

Little did I know, we were being filmed for a Los Angeles news magazine show called "Eye On LA." The United Way people called me later that week and said they also had taken pictures and asked if I'd like some copies. Of course I couldn't say no. We went to the United Way office to select our photos and they asked me if I'd like to go to Barry's United Way Benefit Concert at the Hollywood Bowl. Being that I had his albums, loved his music, but had never been able to go to one of his concerts, I said 'yes,' thanking them endlessly as I was handed four tickets for box seats, eight rows from the stage.

I was at work on that concert Friday when I received a call that Melissa had a fever. I reluctantly had to give away the tickets. A pediatric nurse whom I knew said she'd watch Melissa for me so I could go. Of course, I would have loved going to the concert, but never would have forgiven myself as I knew I'd worry about her the whole time. I took pictures of the tickets lying on my kitchen table and gave them away to my friends at work. I've never been able to attend one of his concerts since, but sure do hope this happens one day just to hear that special song, 'Sweet Melissa, angel of my lifetime, answer to all answers I can find...'

1983 was Melissa's best year. I remember at another one of her checkups the doctors said she wouldn't see her first birthday. She proceeded to make a lie out of that statement as she loved, smiled, and laughed her way through life. She would even hold her little hands together sitting up and clap as we'd sing to Barry Manilow songs at home.

1984 started out as a good year for us. However, in the middle of planning for her 2nd birthday party the beginning of April, she became ill and once again went into Children's Hospital. This would be her last visit. After one month she started deteriorating rapidly as her heart muscle became tissue-paper thin and could no longer work. She spent the last four weeks of her two month stay in ICU, hooked up to God knows what. The hardest part of it all was when I signed the 'No Code' sheet, allowing her to die if she started arresting. I remember my mother sitting in Melissa's hospital room and saying that song came on with Barry Manilow singing 'Could It Be Magic' and seeing a tear roll out of Melissa's eye. My sweet Melissa, born April 14, 1982, died June 5, 1984.

I'll never forget that day I met Barry Manilow. His warmth, caring and sincerity were worth so much to me at that time in my life. It meant more to me than anyone would ever know. I only wish that perhaps somehow, someday, I have the pleasure of looking him in the eyes and telling him this. How simple kind acts of someone could help me through that trying time in my life. Thank you, Barry.

By: Karen Caporali

# Chapter Six

# Even Now

Some Barry Manilow fans have followed his career since he exploded onto the charts in 1974 with what was the beginning of a string of hits. Other fans, some young and some much older, are just now discovering the music of Barry Manilow as he continues to make appearances worldwide while he promotes new material and dazzles his audience with a myriad of his chart-topping singles. Whatever it is that draws a person to his music, thousands of people have decided to take an active role in involving themselves in his career.

Many fans have shared for this book how they got hooked on Barry and his infectious music. In addition, other fans have talked about the feelings they get from his music and his mesmerizing live appearances. All in all, the following fans share how and why they have chosen to include the music and career of Barry Manilow in their busy, daily lives. One thing is for sure, there is no doubt that Barry Manilow has made, and continues to make, a difference in people's lives.

*Although Jessica Whitlock is* most likely not Barry Manilow's youngest fan, she is, however, one of the youngest fans ever to sing "Can't Smile Without You" with Barry in concert. Her shining moment came on December 2, 1997, at the Tampa Bay Performing Arts Center in Tampa, Florida. At just 13 years old, Jessica was selected from a crowd of thousands. Did Barry have any idea how young she was when he chose her? Possibly not. But when Jessica stepped onto the stage, Barry probably knew then that she was younger than the majority of people who have graced the stage for this moment in the past. When Barry asked her age, the entire audience gasped with joy and gave her just that much more encouragement as she was about to partake in her life-changing adventure.

Jessica remembers listening to Barry's songs when she was only three years old. Her father had a vast collection of music which included Barry Manilow's material.

Then, after beginning the third grade, Jessica's parents divorced. Jessica first thought that her young age spared her from the pain of her parents' split, but as the years went by, she found out that she was mistaken. Jessica began to experience behavioral differences and as a result, her grades declined and the stress that overwhelmed her took its toll on her health, requiring her to take massive amounts of stomach medications each night to prevent her from becoming physically ill. While her mother began to date again, her father struggled to keep his family fed. Jessica was soon neglected and became a victim of physical abuse.

By the time Jessica entered the fifth grade, she was getting pretty good at dealing with the stress of a broken home and an abused existence. She simply turned all of her hurt and pain inward. Tell-tale signs of her personal and private destruction began to emerge and Jessica didn't like what she was seeing. But somehow, she couldn't stop herself from doing all of those things she didn't want to do. Jessica began to smoke, she developed anorexia, she started taking drugs, and she inflicted pain on herself which eventually lead to several suicide attempts.

"Then," Jessica explained, "I went back to Mr. Manilow. I slowly regained a sense of who I was, who I wanted to be, where I was going, and what I wanted to do." She started middle school, joined choir, and became an avid Manilow fan. "I smiled again for the first time in years," Jessica said. Jessica still had her share of problems, but because of rediscovering the music of Barry Manilow, she gained an overwhelming confidence that she could overcome each one of them.

And without a doubt, Jessica's opportunity to sing with Barry only solidified the positive course she has chosen to pursue with her young life. This eighth-grader boasts a 3.4 grade point average and takes piano and voice lessons to boot. Above everything else, she keeps a positive attitude.

"Had it not been for Mr. Manilow, Lord knows where I would be right now and I shudder to think of it. But because of him, look where I am and who I've become. Mr. Manilow has made me into a wonderful person; a person who feels, loves, considers, and forgives. For that I cannot thank him enough," Jessica said.

Jessica fills her life with schoolwork, music, books and writing, not to mention the hundreds of fellow Manilow fans she corresponds with through the Internet. Drop Jessica a note at BmanFan3@aol.com or Manifan@webtv.net.

KLBJ-FM is one of the most listened-to rock stations in Austin, Texas. With 100,000 watts, DJs reach an audience of thousands. Demographic studies show that the majority of their listeners are men ranging in age from 25 to 54 years old. And for the many acts that visit the Frank Erwin Jr. Special Events Center, located near the University of Texas in Austin, KLBJ-FM lends a hand in helping promote their appearances.

Much of the entertainment that graces the stage at the Frank Erwin Jr. Special Events Center are rock-n-roll groups or relatively new acts that take the nation by storm, in addition to classic big-name individual artists and groups. When Barry Manilow visited Austin for his November, 1997, performance at the Center, KLBJ-FM once again stepped up to the plate to promote Barry's appearance in any way they could.

Jeff Carrol, Operations Manager at KLBJ-FM, is always in the midst of the excitement when acts roll into town. Barry's upcoming performance was no exception. "They asked if we would be interested in giving away tickets to the show or just announcing the event," said Jeff. "At first, I was hesitant, but thought that our morning show might be able to have some fun with it. Our morning team has a mostly talk show format and hence it reaches a broader base than just the rock listeners. One of the team members is a fan of Barry's so they said they would like to do something."

"Something" is an understatement. KLBJ-FM dove in head-first. Putting their creative minds to work, the KLBJ-FM staff decided that it would be fun to sponsor contests for great ticket give-a-ways which included "look alike," "sound alike," and "tell us why you need to go" types of contests. KLBJ-FM was inundated with contestants.

All the while these contests were taking place, fans from around KLBJ-FM's listening area called the station to request Barry's songs. Keep in mind that this is a rock station. And unless you've musically lived under a rolling stone, you would know that Barry's songs are the antitheses of "rock." Eager to please their listeners, KLBJ-FM's morning hosts, Dudley and Bob with Debra, happily cued up Barry's tunes in conjunction with the contest promotions and ticket give-a-ways. The contests were a hit!

Some of the lucky radio station personnel were able to meet Barry at a record company "meet and greet" while others attended his packed performance. After the concert, the station personnel talked about Barry's performance both on and off the air for days afterwards.

"We don't play any of Mr. Manilow's music in regular rotation," explained Jeff. After witnessing the extreme audience participation and support as Barry's concert approached, perhaps a program change might be considered? Since KLBJ-FM has experienced unrivaled success in the rock arena for over 25 years, it is highly unlikely this would happen.....maybe just one hour of Manilow music a day?

*Dear Barry,*

*Just wanted to say "thank you" for your music. Your music is wonderful and beautiful. It has touched my life in so many ways.*

*A few years back I was going through a really bad time. It seems like my whole world was dark and gray and thought I had no friends. And my marriage was in trouble, my dad was very sick and I had a lot of stressors. A lot of people walked away from me. Thank you Barry. Your music got me through those dark and lonely days.*

*I have met so many new friends. It is so exciting to see and hear you. Keep up the good work, Barry!*

*Love from the dairyland.*

*Vicki Villers*

*Once upon a time* there was a young, ambitious gentleman who was employed by a cutting-edge and aggressive music publishing company. This publishing company, Pocket Full of Tunes, located in New York City, had many high profile musical acts and artists as clients. These were the movers and shakers of the day, the hit machines of the recording industry. Jay Warner, the bright, young executive, matched songs with artists, pitched and licensed the songs to the record companies and their artists and management, and throughout his years of association with the publishing company, he racked up dozens and dozens of popular and famous artist-come-celebrities as clientele. It was the 70s and new recording artists were popping up from everywhere. One new and shining star on the horizon was Barry Manilow, and among others, Pocket Full of Tunes enjoined with Barry to create a special and prosperous relationship.

One day, Jay needed to contact Barry. Something urgent had come up and he was unable to locate Barry's manager, so in that case, Jay needed to get Barry on the phone right away. After searching high and low, Jay and his staff were unable to come up with Barry's personal number. Why now? It was no time to look for a phone number and there was little time to waste. Out of the blue, one of Jay's secretaries mentioned, "Why don't we try the phone book?" Jay's reaction was less than receptive. "Yea, right," Jay scoffed, "Like this star recording artist is going to be in the phone book." Out of sheer desperation, Jay picked up the phone and dialed information. There was a Barry Manilow listed with information.

There couldn't be more than one Barry Manilow, right? That was what Jay was hoping! Jay dialed the number... "Hello?" Sure enough, it was Barry Manilow. After shaking off the disbelief, Jay proceeded with the business at hand. "Barry," Jay said, "I have to talk to you about this project, but before I do, I have to know something. Why in the hell are you, after a number one record, still listed in the New York phone book and with the phone company?" Barry's response was not what Jay had expected. "I just love to get the calls from the fans so I never bothered to take it out of the phone book," Barry replied.

Jay and Barry's professional relationship lasted from "Mandy" to "I Write the Songs," but their personal relationship has endured throughout the years. Jay still fondly recalls Barry's early performances following such acts as Andy Kaufman as he worked the small clubs and theaters. Jay was always behind Barry's career, 110% and that hasn't changed either. "Barry, one, was unique, and, two, was supremely likeable," said Jay.

Jay Warner is president of National League Music, Inc. located in California and author of several books including *How to Have Your Hit Song Published*, which incidentally, was endorsed on the back cover by none other than Barry Manilow.

*Some people only dream* of having a job where they develop video games for a living. This is not a fantasy for May Yam. It is her life. Not only does she put her education in Computer Science to good use at work, she has combined her love for computers and her love for Barry Manilow into what is commonly known within the Manilow circles as the *ManiWeb*.

From May's first introduction to the Internet in 1995, she began searching for any information she could find on Barry Manilow and to her astonishment, she found nothing. With today's surge of Internet popularity, this seems hard to believe. So, May made her decision to marry her two loves — Barry and the Internet. Therefore, May pioneered what was the very first Barry Manilow website on the Internet.

What is the *ManiWeb*? Go to any computer with Internet access and type: http://www.netfusion.com/maniweb/ in the address box. Welcome to the immensely popular, frequently hit site of the *ManiWeb*. Navigating around this site, you will see May's creative handiwork. May combines articles, poems, and stories submitted by Barry's fans along with her use of graphics and *voila*. You also can't miss the many sumptuous photos of "the man" himself. Where does May get these gorgeous pictures? Why, the fans, of course. Barry's many fans and May herself unselfishly share their personal photos that they have snapped throughout the years, all just for visiting the *ManiWeb*.

It was a personal desire of May's to develop this website about Barry Manilow and his career. It initially took May three months to organize the site. She designed the navigational bars, backgrounds, and graphics. Next, May obtained server space and a domain name. Then she submitted the site to numerous search engines. The *ManiWeb* became publicly accessible and before she knew it, fans by the hundreds were contacting May about the site. Fans from around the world were e-mailing her to tell her how Barry had been their driving force from childhood. Fans from Japan, Thailand and Germany even told her how they learned English from Barry's lyrics. May knew she was on to something. Articles and poems turned into complete sections on literature, pen pals, buying and selling opportunities and survey and voting opportunities. She even began including weekly trivia, crosswords, name scrambles and puzzles. The "Barry Bug" had definitely caught on.

*ManiWeb* has been growing by leaps and bounds since it began. May recently added a Manilow Postcard site for fans to converse with each other through personalized photos of Barry. With over 1,000 images and 2,000 pages of text, she added a search engine to help fans navigate the site more easily. After all, she wants the fans to feel at ease every time they come home to the *ManiWeb*.

May has gained well-deserved respect by her peers; fans and organizations alike. *ManiWeb* has won several web authoring awards for ease of navigation, content, and graphics. *ManiWeb* has even received recognition from *USA Today*, CNN, Net Radio, *The Web Magazine*, and AT&T.

So, after receiving these kudos, May is hardly relaxing and reveling in her accomplishments. She is constantly thinking of new ways to make the *ManiWeb* a pleasant and popular site. May is currently tidying up the details for on-line chats, seasonal Manilow postcards with animation and audio, a message center, more interactive games and even exclusive interviews and information to satisfy the hungry Manilow fans.

"Through *ManiWeb*, I strive to stay true to that which is 'Barry Manilow,' promoting both the Music and the Man. This labor of love is motivated by my desire to 'give back' a little of what Barry has given me. May you receive as much joy from navigating *ManiWeb* as I have received in designing and maintaining it" said May. You can e-mail May at myam@netfusion.com.

*When Donna Gosselin was* 15 years old she wrote Barry Manilow a letter. Then, when she turned 17 years old, Donna mailed another letter to Barry. After reading Barry's autobiography in 1996, she wrote him one more time. Did she ever expect to get a response from Barry? Not really. Donna simply wanted to let Barry know how much she admired him and how much his music has meant to her throughout the years. In all truthfulness, that letter mailed in 1996 was the last one she imagined writing to Barry. But, as we know, the future can't be told and Donna had no idea that her future was going to involve receiving *The Complete Collection...and Then Some*, Barry's box set, for a birthday present. What Donna also couldn't predict was that her 4 year old daughter, Hayley, would fall head over heels for Barry Manilow.

One day, Donna and Hayley sat down to watch the video that was included in the box set. Donna truly believed that the pleasure would be all hers and Hayley would sit quietly with her as she took a trip down memory lane watching Barry. Attentive and observant Hayley had other plans. Hayley watched the video, unmistakably taking a shine to Barry. For two solid months, Hayley reenacted parts of the video. Whenever bath-time rolled around, Hayley, using the tub as her private stage, could be heard singing "Copacabana" with Barbie and Ken as her backup act.

"One day," Donna recalled, "Hayley drew a picture of a man with a really big nose and told me it was a picture of Barry. She asked me if I would give it to him when I went to see him." Donna was going to Barry's concert in San Antonio in November, 1997. As Donna tried to reason with 4 year old Hayley, it broke her heart as she explained that she would not be able to give Barry her picture in person. With the ingenious and ingenuity of a 4 year old, Hayley looked up at her Mom with her big puppy-dog brown eyes and said rather matter-of-factly, "Well, mail it to him." What parent could resist?

So, Donna wrote Barry one more time, but this time the letter took on a completely different feeling. She told Barry about his 4 year old fan and how she became enamored with him by watching the video. She had Hayley sign her own name, they sealed the letter including a photo of Hayley with the drawing she had made of Barry and they mailed it to the Barry Manilow International Fan Club (BMIFC) in California. "I figured it would suffer the same fate my previous letters to him had suffered," explained Donna. Was Donna ever wrong!

In February, 1998, an envelope came addressed to Hayley from Stiletto Management. "Inside was a very nice letter from Marc Hulett and an autographed picture of Barry," said Donna. The photo was signed, "Hayley, Love Barry Manilow." According to Donna, you have never seen a 4 year old jump for joy as Hayley did. Honestly, Donna was just short of hyperventilating herself. In true 4 year old puppy-love fashion, Hayley danced around repeatedly, gloating, "He loves me, he loves me!" Even Donna's husband, an admitted non-Barry fan, was impressed with Barry's gesture.

Donna snapped a photo of Hayley with her autographed photo of Barry and sent it along with a thank you note to him. "Who knows," Donna said, "maybe someday she will get to meet him…and I better be there with her when she does!"

*If you found that* you needed to juggle your schedule around three times to attend a concert that had to be rescheduled three times, would you do it? For Barry Manilow fans, this question needs minimal consideration. John Graham, Director of the Frank Erwin Center in Austin, Texas, would have to agree because he witnessed it.

Barry was scheduled to perform at the Frank Erwin Center to promote his recent release, *Summer of '78*. Thousands of tickets were sold for this performance. And on this special day for the Texas fans, Barry went through his tour-routine motions. But something was not quite right. Going into the 4:00 PM sound check, Barry realized that his voice, the voice that those thousands were anxiously anticipating that evening, was in imminent danger. A doctor was called in and sure enough, Barry had bronchitis. The show couldn't go on…at least for that evening. Being the consummate professional, he rescheduled the show for the following night. The fans were notified of the change and cheerfully, they made plans to come back.

But the next day, it soon became clear that Barry would not be in any shape to perform. Once again, the fans were informed that the show would be postponed. Because a double cancellation has happened only one other time in Barry's career, the fans began to get concerned not necessarily concerned about getting their money back or rearranging their schedules one more time, they were more worried about Barry's health. In John Graham's nine years with the Frank Erwin Center he has encountered a multitude of fans. John, however, was genuinely struck by these fans' thoughtfulness. "The Manilow fans were sad the show was canceled, but they were more upset and genuinely concerned about Barry and his health," said John. "If it would have been any other group, those fans who showed up would have been a lot more upset because they were put out. Manilow's fans were only concerned about him. That really says something."

John has had the privilege of working with hundreds of entertainers throughout his career and he has witnessed the fan following that trails each act. But, he is particularly complimentary toward Barry's fans. "I think the closest fan base I've seen to Manilow's is Neil Diamond's," John said. "There's a similarity in the time frame when they became popular and the fan age demographics are the same. Manilow and Diamond fans share a similar kind of fervor for their favorite artist. It's really something to see. It is obvious these fans have developed a love affair with Barry Manilow and they've hung onto it over the years."

No doubt about it, Barry's performances have changed over the years and John has been privy to the modifications because of the unique role that he fills at the Frank Erwin Center. He has been involved with two of Barry's large stage productions, a smaller more theater-like show and the *Summer of '78* performance. "Back in the early 80s, Manilow's productions were huge and extravagant with a rotating stage and 13,000 to 15,000 in the audience," John recalled. "Now his concerts seem to be smaller and more intimate."

But John believes that Manilow himself has changed very little, remaining true to the style the fans expect and have become accustomed to. "Barry Manilow hasn't changed," observed John. "He still looks like Barry Manilow. He's still singing songs like Barry Manilow. He's still delivering the product that brought him the fans in the beginning. Now his die-hard fans are bringing their children to concerts to see him. He may not be getting the same airplay he once did, but Barry Manilow definitely has the staying power.

"He is still giving his fans the music they want to hear. His fans appreciate that. And, Manilow respects his fans by doing that. You know, there have been artists who flip-flop around with their musical style to keep up with what's popular, and the hard-core fans felt left behind and betrayed. Manilow hasn't done that."

The scheduled concert took place on November 20, 1997, with over 5,250 people were in attendance. John Graham was pleased by Barry Manilow's commitment and return to the Frank Erwin Center. "We planned for this concert a total of three times due to his illness, so I guess the third time is the charm," John said with a grin.

*Pamela Jansen's introduction to* Barry Manilow's music happened as a joke. When Pam was a teenager, she involved herself in her high school choir. Classical and jazz were the genres Pam and her choir friends enjoyed most. Actually, they loathed pop music. "We were extremely snooty about our music," explained Pam. So, when Pam turned sweet 16, her mother decided to throw a party for her inviting some of her relatives, buddies from her church and from her school choir.

Her choir pals showed up at the party and brought Pam a gift. Pam was thrilled as she began opening the flat, square package. Pam just knew the contents would contain the Mozart recording by the Academy of St. Anthony In The Fields that she so desperately wanted. Pam couldn't believe her eyes when she unwrapped the gift to find the *Barry Manilow I* album staring back at her. Her pals reveled in Pam's apparent disappointment, hooting and hollering at their success in finding the best gag gift of the day, perhaps of the century. Pam looked up from gazing at the Manilow album and asked the monumental question, "Barry-WHO?"

After all her guests went home, Pam retreated to her bedroom to go through her many gifts. She picked up the Manilow album to take a closer look. Reading through the song titles, her attention was drawn to "Could It Be Magic," which was based on a Chopin prelude. Curiosity got the better of Pam and she placed the round piece of black vinyl on her stereo. "From that moment on my life was never the same," explained Pam. "Could It Be Magic" became her favorite song, and to this very day, it still is.

A few months later, it was Pam's turn to get back at her choir pals. For Christmas gifts, she wanted to return the favor and find the most obnoxious and annoying gifts she could find to place under their festively decorated trees. She knew just the store to visit for those gifts. Pam entered the store and began browsing. Out of the corner of her eye, she noticed a huge poster of which the subject seemed to be staring at her. Turning to see who was on the poster, she was blown away when she discovered it was Barry Manilow. "He was wearing a white suit and leaning against a foil background," Pam said. "The look on his face was so sexy!"

The next thing she knew there was a loud crash and she turned to find that a display of fiber-optic lamps had tumbled over, bounced into a million directions and smashed into other displays, trashing the store. Apparently, Pam was so enthralled with the poster of Barry that she, unknowingly, backed into the display. The store clerk rushed over to check on Pam and begin cleaning up the mess. Pam apologized over and over again to the clerk and instead of getting a verbal whipping, Pam was surprised when the clerk calmly told her, "Don't worry, Hon, this has been happening ever since we put up that Manilow poster." Needless to say, Pam walked out of the store with a new poster that day.

Pam's over 20 year journey enjoying the music and following the career of Barry Manilow has rewarded her with many joys. She has made many friends from her various travels to Manilow concerts, conventions and club parties. She has also been introduced to a variety of music that she otherwise may not have explored on her own. Most of all, she sticks with Barry because of his apparent appreciation for his fans. "All of us, large and small, loud and quiet, he cares about us, our lives, our families, and so on," Pam explained. "He takes time to communicate with us, not only in music, but through the BMIFC (Barry Manilow International Fan Club) as well. I just can't imagine what my life would be like if I had never received that gag gift from my fellow choir members."

*Sabrina Lowd has been* a Barry Manilow fan for over 17 years. She was first introduced to his music by her best friend's mother. Even though Sabrina has listened to Barry's music on and off throughout the years, it wasn't until after attending one of his concerts that she began to take a more serious approach to his career, and her life.

1997 was a real turning point in Sabrina's life partially due to a Barry Manilow concert she attended in Atlanta, Georgia. "I guess as I am getting older, too, you start to reflect a little bit more on what you've done and what you haven't done and where you want to go and the things you want to do that you realize that you really haven't done," explained Sabrina. "I guess that is what that concert did for me. It made me think about things that I keep postponing and saying 'Oh, I'm going to do it one of these days' and then realize that, gosh, I'm 31 and I'm still saying that."

After the concert, Sabrina began surfing the net to get more information on Barry. She had no idea about all of the Barry Manilow fan clubs until she logged on. In this process of learning about Barry via the net, she thought it would be a fun project to develop her own web page. Being a relatively new programmer at that time, she overcame the learning curve and developed: http://www.flpanhandle.com/sabrina/BMFC. One day, Sabrina got a note from a fan who was starting a new Barry Manilow Fan Club and asked her if she would be interested in developing the site for the club. Sabrina felt honored that she liked her new site enough to ask and obliged. The Somewhere In The South (SITS) Barry Manilow Fan Club site was born. "It has been my goal," said Sabrina, "to try to make our site as enjoyable as possible for other Barry fans. Designing this web site has been one of the most exciting and satisfying projects I have ever done."

Sabrina has jumped into the SITS fan club with both feet and is proud of their accomplishments. She also dotes on the new-found friends she has made since she has re-focused her sights on Barry's music. "I have met many wonderful people and made some very good friends through Barry and his music," said Sabrina. "The wonderful thing about our fan club is that it has brought many people together not only to enjoy Barry's music but to also contribute to our communities through charity work."

Not long ago, Sabrina acquired a keyboard and started developing her new passion; creating midis of Barry's music to add to her Barry Midi Site on the Internet. "This is my small way of sharing his music with others who appreciate and enjoy it as much as I do," Sabrina said.

Sabrina has accomplished a lot since Barry's July 20, 1997, concert. The outlook she has on her own life has changed dramatically. "Watching him on stage, listening to him and his music really made me rethink my life. I realized I had put my dreams on the back burner, too afraid to venture out of my safe little world I had created for myself. As a result of this revelation, I have started writing and playing the piano again," Sabrina said. "My days are much happier and more fulfilling now than they have ever been."

If you are interested in developing a web site for your Barry Manilow Fan Club, your business, a personal site, or a site for other entertainer's fan clubs, please contact Sabrina at sabrina@flpanhandle.com or visit her web site.

*Cheryl Liebowitz has listened* to Barry's music for over 20 years. She purchases his new releases each time they hit the shelves and for 10 years, she has attended his concerts.

Cheryl was born in New York City and now makes her home in Palm Harbor, Florida. Cheryl and her husband are very successful business people, owning a multi-million dollar electronics company and several restaurants. When they want to relax, Cheryl and her husband take exotic cruises and vacation all over the world. But, one of their most enjoyable forms of entertainment is attending a Barry Manilow concert.

Cheryl and her husband always make an event of seeing Barry in concert. They go to a nice restaurant for a romantic dinner, then, off to the concert. The beat takes them away when Barry performs one of their favorites, "Copacabana," and Cheryl has even been known to try her luck at getting chosen to sing "Can't Smile Without You" with Barry.

"We always make a night of it. Al takes me to dinner, we see the show, and then go home for pleasure, inspired by his concert," Cheryl admitted.

*Whatever you do, don't* call Amanda Jo Avery, "Mandy." "I hate being called 'Mandy,'" Amanda stated, "I have all my life. Weird isn't it? I guess I don't mind too much anymore, but, I introduce myself as 'Amanda', always!". Being that many Manilow fans first fell in love with Barry Manilow and his music because of his wildly popular song, "Mandy," many fans only dream of having that name. So, they do the next best thing; they name their daughters "Mandy" or sometimes their pets. But, this whole Barry Manilow fan-thing is all new to Amanda because at 21 years old, she is just discovering Barry Manilow's music and career, making friendships and new findings about herself along the way.

Amanda is a budding musician herself. Being compelled to make music is not new to her, but, being profoundly inspired by Barry Manilow is. For an entire year, Amanda experienced what can be one of the most devastating occurrences that can happen to a musician/songwriter. She suffered from severe writer's block. For some, it takes a particular circumstance to happen in one's life before this condition can be overcome. Unbeknownst to Amanda, it would take her very first Barry Manilow concert to propel her from her dusty, parched condition.

"I thought I'd lost all my inspiration for writing," explained Amanda. "It had been over a year since I had written anything decent, except for one depressing song that I wrote in England. Funny thing. England was the happiest time of my life!" As luck would again have it, one Barry Manilow concert changed Amanda's life.

It happened in April, 1997, in Grand Rapids, Michigan. Amanda knew little to nothing about Barry Manilow or the music he has made throughout the years. She wasn't even very familiar with "Copacabana", the song almost everyone knows whether they like Manilow's music or not. But, she agreed to go to the concert with her friend. "He won the tickets from a radio station and the seats were awful," Amanda recalled. "But, when I got there, it didn't matter. Mr. Manilow had me with the first note he sang!" She knew the feelings she had experienced during the concert were quite rare. "I was in awe. I had never had my emotions taken to so many places in just three hours," Amanda said. "It was a 'thunderbolt' for me and I will never forget that night, nor will I ever be the same."

After the concert, Amanda described that she was "in a daze." She woke up the next morning felling something very strange. She went to the college where she once attended and headed straight for the piano room. She is not a piano player, hunting and pecking mostly by ear, but, she knew that what was about to emerge from the depths of her soul was going to take place through the white and black keys. She sat down on the piano bench and began singing a melody. Then, something very beautiful began to happen; lyrics came spilling from her lips. Three hours later, Amanda had finished her piece. As if she had just experienced a clean, warm, spring rain, her year of drought was finally over. She sang the song she had just written and cried. "I sat in that room crying for half an hour because I had written and because it wasn't at all like before...it was passionate and full of emotion," Amanda rejoiced. That was the beginning of Amanda's three month writing fury.

"Through discovering Mr. Manilow, I discovered confidence in myself and my dreams, passion, and the way music really feels. I wasn't afraid to feel it anymore. I craved it," explained Amanda. "Before Mr. Manilow, I was afraid to realize my dreams and had no direction. But now, I have recorded my first demo CD. Mr. Manilow's genius broke me from a year long writer's block and essentially turned me into the singer/songwriter I am today. Mr. Manilow showed me in that one night to feel the music and listen to it rather than just hear it. Though it has always been in my blood, I don't think I would have realized any of my musical dreams without his encouraging words, passion, and wisdom. I am a better singer, better song-writer, and a better person for having discovered Mr. Manilow, as a person and a musical genius."

*It has been a little* over 10 years now since Julie Campbell first heard Barry Manilow's music. Julie was always teased in school for her musical taste. Sometimes now, she gets teased by her co-workers. But, at 21 years old, Julie feels more capable of handling the ribbing and responds with pride and confidence.

Although Julie can't pinpoint the exact place and time in which she first heard a Barry Manilow song, she does recall the event that signed, sealed, and delivered her into full-fledged Manilow devotion. In 1989 during the *Big Fun* Tour, Julie and her parents took in a concert near their home. Julie had never seen Barry in person before. "I was more shocked than anything else," Julie remembered. In 1989, Julie was only 12 years old. Just imagine the awe that took over when Barry Manilow, big as life, took to the stage, opened his mouth, and that big, tantalizing, beckoning voice, touched Julie right where she sat. Julie was enveloped, captured, and hooked.

Now, this is a good, clean, safe addiction that has stood the test of time and one in which Julie has no plans of kicking. On one other concert occasion, Julie was blessed with 2$^{nd}$ row seats. For a fan of any entertainer, this is a true privilege. Julie was a few years older and wiser, but no more prepared for her pending "date" with Manilow than the first time. "The time I saw him walk out on stage, I nearly passed out," Julie described. "It was so real and so emotional I could hardly stand it. He was a lot taller than I imagined. And when he sang that first note, I was history. I did not move until the concert was over. I was overwhelmed with his power."

These days when Julie attends Barry's concerts, she and her good friend travel together. When she is at home, she fires up her computer and involves herself in Manilow-related sites where she has befriended some very special people. When she first started searching for Manilow "on-line," she was amazed at the number of people who love Barry and follow his career, "not just people who have a record here and there, but, these people have a collection of his music and memorabilia," said Julie.

"Today when somebody asks me, 'You like Barry Manilow?', I respond proudly, "Nope. I love Barry Manilow! Always have and always will,'" said Julie.

"*Barry's music speaks to* the core of my soul because I have gone through situations like the ones he sings about. Everyone has. I know that many singers sing songs about love, breakups, etc., but, Barry really sounds like it happened to him. He's like a good friend who's been there and can be a shoulder to cry on. When you are down, Barry is there to listen and his songs are his reply," explained George Krieger.

George, a social worker specializing in child welfare, recently completed his Masters degree and in the Fall of 1997 began coursework for his Ph.D. In between work and school, George dotes on his young daughter. All of this combined doesn't leave George much spare time for himself. But when he does take time out for a little R & R, George likes to sing and listen to music.

George was first introduced to Barry's music around 1978. That is when he first heard "Could It Be Magic." "I was eight at the time and I had just gotten a tape recorder for my birthday. I taped the song repeatedly on a tape so that I could listen to it over and over. It was just one of those songs I never got tired of," George explained. George's appreciation for Barry's music and talents grew and grew.

"I most relate to Barry in the way that his songs are so full of emotions that most men, and many women, are ashamed to sing about," George described. "Even with that said, sometimes I want to say to him, 'Barry! Snap out of it! Get over her already!' You know, songs like 'Even Now' and 'Looks Like We Made It.' But then I realize that there are times I think about my first love, with whom I thought I would spend the rest of my life, and I am glad he sings those songs."

George believes in the powerful lyrics of Barry's songs so deeply that he has even sung some of those songs to people in order to express feelings that he couldn't put into words. "Barry has helped me through some rough times, times when I was alone and it's always easier to be with someone who understands. Barry helps me express my feelings, soothes my wounds, and lets me grow through the hurt. He continues to be one of my favorite performers, if not *the* favorite," said George.

'Twas the night before Christmas and all through the house, not a creature was stirring...except for Tina Triesky. House rules were that her mom and dad were to be the first ones to venture downstairs on Christmas mornings. Young Tina wasn't real hip on these rules and was determined to make her wishes known.

Tina was about 12 years old when she figured out a way to inform the "sleeping beauties" that the hour of reckoning had arrived and it was time they got up and opened packages. 8:00 AM was the magic hour when Tina was allowed to emerge from her room to make a run for the tree. Like a hawk, she watched the clock. When the little hand was on "8" and the big hand reached "12," Tina sounded reveille. Blasting throughout the upstairs corridors came the unmistakable sounds of "Daybreak." Needless to say, everybody woke up, and fast. Tina's sister was not impressed with this display.

Tina recalled that she did not get in trouble for waking the household this way. Actually, her family fondly remembers the event with a chuckle when they think about it today.

## by Jill Prince

*For about 12 years*, I had been a solo Manilow fan—I traveled, attended concerts, etc., all by myself. Then, in the fall of '95, during a particularly rough part of my life, I bought my first computer and began trying to track down any Manilow sites I could find. I eventually made my way to the Prodigy online service and the Barry bulletin board there. I would read through the messages, and they sounded like a friendly group, but I was too scared to jump in and post.

One day, one of the girls posted that her sister had made her a Barry webpage as a Christmas gift and invited everyone to have a look at it. I did and discovered that she lived just a couple of hours away from me in South Carolina. There was a place on the website to e-mail her, which I did—and that e-mail quite literally changed my life. She immediately wrote back and encouraged me to post on the board and to also join them at their regular Friday night chat. In January of '96 I put my first tentative post on the board, joining in some Barry trivia game they were playing. Later that week I made my first appearance at Chat.

This group of people was so friendly and so welcoming and so much fun! I found myself sitting at my computer laughing hysterically every Friday night. Before long, I felt like one of the gang. It seemed as if everyone had been friends forever, but in fact, other than a few exceptions here and there, no one had ever even met. So, when Barry's May concerts at the Mirage in Las Vegas were announced, everyone decided to go. I did not see any way that I could possibly make the trip, as I had already made plans to attend Barry's UK shows in April, and my budget couldn't afford to do both. But, these gals were insistent and as everyone quickly found out, my arms are easily twisted.

So, off we went to Vegas—a bunch of strangers. My friends and family thought I was nuts—in fact, I thought I was nuts! I was rooming with two girls I had never laid eyes on in my life and whom I only knew as words on a computer monitor. The possibilities for catastrophe were endless—bringing together a large group of women, from all different backgrounds, areas of the country, and age groups, who had never met each other. What on earth were we thinking? But, what went on that weekend, we still marvel at today. It was one of those unique experiences in your life that you know you were lucky to be a part of and that will never happen again. I had never felt so close to a group of people so quickly in my life.

This group is now one of the most important things in my life. The friendships we made on that trip have endured and strengthened. We have shared some horrible tragedies and some incredible highs—some hilarious road trips and some very special Barry moments—and we've done it all together. The bond has extended far beyond our common love for Barry and we have become an important part of each others' daily lives. They are truly like a second family to me and having them in my life has been one of the best blessings I have ever received. And we have Barry to thank for it. After 12 years of doing this stuff solo, now I can't even enjoy myself at a show without having one of them to share it with. I only wish we'd found each other sooner.

*When Jan Taylor was* growing up, she watched Barry's TV specials and purchased his albums, but she never seemed to be able to save up enough cash to purchase concert tickets. But, that has changed. She now enjoys attending Barry's concerts even though she still meticulously plans for ticket expenses around the parental responsibilities of raising her four children.

Jan's very first Barry concert came in January, 1989. Her husband purchased the tickets as her Christmas present and sneakily tucked the tickets inside the wrapper of a chocolate candy bar and placed them in the bottom of her Christmas stocking.

One pre-concert snowy evening, the Taylors left their home for an evening out. They gave their final instructions to the babysitter and blissfully exited into the night. One tiny bit of information Mr. Taylor neglected to give the babysitter was to keep their dog away from Mrs. Taylor's Christmas stocking. Sometime during that evening, the babysitter let the dog in the house and in the mayhem of attending to the children, the babysitter lost track of the dog's whereabouts.

Like a homing pigeon, the dog zeroed in on Jan's Christmas stocking, sensing that there was chocolate inside. Tearing through Jan's stocking, the dog delighted in the sweet and tasty treat nestled, ever-so-carefully in the toe of the stocking. Fortunately, for both the dog and Jan, only a portion of the candy was eaten and the concert tickets were left perfectly intact.

The concert was a much-needed respite for Jan. When Barry sang, "Please Don't Be Scared," she sat in her seat and cried. Jan felt as though the Opera House was completely empty and Barry was singing only to her. The song was exactly what she needed to hear as she was going though some difficulties in her life during that time.

Jan is thankful to her loving husband for thinking of concert tickets for her Christmas gift. He knew that seeing Barry would take Jan away if only for a short time. She is also relieved that her dog didn't have any reactions to the chocolate he wolfed down that evening and also that the tickets emerged unscathed. You can just imagine what must have been running through Jan's head as she handed the concert venue ticket-taker her prized Manilow tickets with melted chocolate on them!

*Just imagine . . . you are* 12 years old and you are sitting two feet in front of your television, tape recorder primed, waiting for Barry's first TV special to start. You anxiously await the music to begin, the credits to roll, and for Barry to appear. Your fingers are poised over the "record" and "start" buttons. For some, this image seems extremely far-fetched. Come on, recording a TV program? For others (and you know who you are), this description could be you! It was JoAnn Bernardi too. JoAnn has always been inspired by Barry and his music and like many other fans, she fondly remembers those childhood recording sessions in the pre-VCR days. Never in JoAnn's wildest dreams, as she laid her 12 year old head on her pillow at nights, would she have thought she would bake cookies for a Barry Manilow International Fan Club (BMIFC) sponsored contest and win.

After Christmas in 1994, JoAnn, of Rochester, New York, and her sister found themselves jetting to Palm Springs to attend a Barry Manilow convention. This was the opportunity of a lifetime for JoAnn and she wasn't going to miss it. She was determined to make the most of her trip. She treated herself to an afternoon at a local spa, visited the San Diego zoo, went to the ocean, and wound up in Las Vegas on New Year's eve. Nestled in between her extra curricular activities, she had a job to do.

JoAnn has a passion for baking. In fact, another dream of hers is to start her own cookie company. She had perfected her chocolate chip cookie recipe and wanted to try them out on Barry. Why not? Cookies in tow, JoAnn approached an usher at one of the concerts and asked if she could get them to Barry, so the usher showed her to the stage door. According to JoAnn, Barry told his audience that evening that he has the sweetest fans. Hearing that comment, JoAnn was certain he had received the cookies.

The next day, the cookie contest was held prior to a question and answer session Barry would be hosting. JoAnn didn't know what she was more nervous for, the cookie contest, or seeing Barry, face-to-face. Just being that close to him in the same room was enough for her.

Before Barry arrived for the Q & A session, the cookie bake-off winner was announced. JoAnn couldn't believe it. Shaking, she accepted her prize and sat back down, astonished that she had won. But, the best was yet to come. And, as if winning a baking contest wasn't enough, she had knock-out seats for the Q & A.

JoAnn found herself 12 feet away from Barry. At one point, Barry even stood right next to her table as he looked at dolls some fans had made of him and his back-up singers. Her sister, Susie took plenty of pictures, which was a good thing, since JoAnn was practically in a trance.

JoAnn left the convention even more inspired to pursue her dream of baking. She has attended classes in business and has sold her cookies to a local bed and breakfast as well as other eateries in her area. She is consistently experimenting with new recipes including low-fat and sugar free versions of her favorites. "Barry has always inspired us to go after our dreams," said JoAnn, "and mine was to make a living selling cookies."

To order a batch of her award-winning chocolate chip cookies or to try others in her line e-mail JoAnn at JoAnn617@aol.com.

Darlene Schwartz and the "Maniloonies" getting ready to board the
"Maniloonie Fun Bus"

*How long have you* been a Manilow fan? For Darlene Schwartz of Northbrook, Illinois, since "Mandy" began soaring the charts in 1975. But, it wasn't until 1990 that Darlene became an active fan. She always purchased Barry's latest releases, but, because she was busy raising her family and helping her husband through dental school, she was not able to muster up the extra time or cash to become more involved in Barry's career. All of that changed in 1990 when Darlene attended her first Barry concert.

"I was totally unaware of how immense this 'Manilow world' is and what is out there and I wanted to explore it," said Darlene. Explore it she

No distance is too far for Darlene to travel for another Barry Manilow concert. From Chicago, to Europe, to New York City's Radio City Music Hall, she's been there.

did. She started by going to concerts and while at one of them, she bought a program. On the back of the program she discovered the contact information for the BMIFC, Barry Manilow International Fan Club, located in California. She joined this fan club and when she received her membership packet, she was ecstatic when she read about local fan clubs scattered throughout the US and abroad.

Not only did Darlene contact the local clubs in Illinois, she wrote to all of the fan clubs listed in the BMIFC packet! "I am an all or nothing girl," explained Darlene. Forty-six fan clubs responded to her, so, she joined all 46 clubs.

Darlene said, "At this stage of my life, this is a priority for me. I have waited all these years and raised my family, now it is my time." Since 1990, Darlene has narrowed down her club involvement, but, she remains true to Barry Manilow. Jack, her husband of more than 25 years, plays along with her hobby. In fact, during the month of January, 1998, Darlene visited her good friend, Marcy, in the UK (whom she met through a fan club, of course) and traveled from town to town, concert to concert (Barry's, naturally) with a UK based Manilow fan club, the "Maniloonies." Darlene found out that the Maniloonies were going to charter a bus for the month-long string of shows and she knew this would be the perfect opportunity to see her friends Marcy and Barry.

She saw nine shows in 18 days, and she has memories she will treasure.

*One day in 1975,* while she was browsing through her local record store, Barry Manilow captured Lyn Arnold's heart. Lyn was at the store to purchase the *Barry Manilow II* album for a boyfriend's birthday. Unfortunately, the store was fresh out of that copy. What the store did have in stock was the *Barry Manilow I* album from which the recording of "Could It Be Magic" came pulsating through the store speakers. "I thought it was the most beautiful song I had ever heard," Lyn said. "Needless to say, the purchase I made that day was the *Barry Manilow I* album and it was for me!"

In the summer of 1980, Lyn got her first chance to see Barry perform live at the Concord Pavilion in Concord, California. It was a beautiful summer evening at the Pavilion with the stars overhead. Lyn thought that evening was about as close as a person could get to heaven on earth; sitting outdoors under the stars and listening to Barry's beautiful voice. During that time, it was the *Barry Manilow Live* album (that Lyn played until she practically wore the grooves out of the record.) "I believe that album captures the essence of Barry's humor on stage, and, for me, finally seeing him perform live was like watching that album come to life," explained Lyn. After that night in California, she knew going to Barry's concerts was going to become a regular event in her life.

The *Barry Manilow I* album is still one of Lyn's treasured possessions and it remains in perfect condition with the original plastic cover with the sticker that says, "Features the Great Song, Could It Be Magic." "For me," said Lyn, " 'Could It Be Magic' is Barry's signature song. It's the type of beautiful song that wraps around your soul and carries you away. I've often told people close to me that that's the song I want to be listening to whenever it's my time to go!"

*In 1978 Lynne Hazard* was in the 8th grade and like most young girls her age, Lynne's bedroom walls were covered with pictures and posters of her favorite hunks. On one side of her room were pictures of the Bay City Rollers and the other side was plastered with pictures of Barry Manilow. As the years went by, the BCR disappeared as more Barry photos began taking their place. Eventually, her bedroom walls were a homage to her heartthrob, Barry. Her mom assured Lynne that it was a phase she was going through and that she'd soon grow out of it. Although her bedroom is no longer a shrine to Barry (her husband probably has something to do with that), Lynne has not "outgrown" loving Barry Manilow and his music.

During those teenage-crush years, Lynne developed an annual tradition of baking a birthday cake for Barry. Each year when June 17 rolled around, Lynn gathered all the ingredients, prepared the pans, whipped up the frostings and forbade anyone to help her bake Barry's cake. Not too many years went by before this yearly ritual became an "understood" event within her household. Her mom would go out and buy the cake mix in advance, knowing little Lynne would be anxiously awaiting the happy day. Lynne was meticulous about how she decorated the cake, too. She had a special tube she'd carefully fill with rich, colorful icing and she scrolled, "Happy Birthday Barry" in perfect penmanship. Her finishing touches to the cake always included candles.

To this day, Lynne continues to bake a cake on June 17 in honor of Barry's birthday. She doesn't elaborately decorate the cake anymore, but, in her heart, she knows the significance of this tradition. Her mom even says that Barry is like a member of their family because he has been a "part" of it for so many years. "I almost feel as if we've grown up together," Lynne said about she and Barry. "I grew up through my childhood with him and he grew up through his adulthood."

Lynne isn't completely void of her adolescent ways. "In fact," Lynne said, "there's a Barry Manilow calendar on my bedroom wall!" What does her husband think about that? Lynne respects their relationship, but she continues to remind him that "Barry came along way before he did!" For Lynne, her husband can live with that. He even agreed to have "The Best of Me" sung at their wedding.

*If it weren't for* receiving an album for a gift that she didn't like, Ana Cristina Ignatti might not be the major Barry Manilow fan that she is today. In 1981, Ana Cristina's Aunt gave her an album as a gift. Ana Cristina was, shall we say, less than thrilled with the gift and she decided to exchange the album for another. At the time, Barry's hit, "I Made It Through The Rain" was climbing the charts and Ana Cristina adored the song so much, she replaced her gift with a Manilow album. She brought the album home and began listening to it over and over. Ana Cristina was so enamored with Barry's voice, she began to buy all of his albums. And this was just the start of what Ana Cristina refers to as an "endless friend-ship" with Barry, his music and career.

There was just one small problem; Ana Cristina could not understand English. Ana Cristina lives in a small town near the state capital of Sao Paulo in Brazil. Ana Cristina had some English grammar in school, but not enough to be able to speak or understand it. So, Barry became Ana Cristina's tutor. "I want to tell you that everything I know how to speak and write in English, I learned with Barry," Ana Cristina said. "I use to (and I still do) listen to his songs over and over again until I have understood what he was singing. I wrote the words and for my surprise, I was right most of the time."

Ana Cristina has never had the opportunity to see Barry in concert, but, that doesn't stop her from dreaming about the experience. Until then, Ana Cristina keeps in touch with several Manilow fans and keeps up with Barry's activities via the Internet and through countless phone calls. "Barry is my inspiration and I love his songs because they seem to help me in each moment of my life. He is a wonderful and amazing person," said Ana Cristina. "Now I express all my feelings through Barry's songs. Thank God I know Barry and I thank Barry. Because of him I have met many good and special friends. All my love to them."

Ana Cristina welcomes other Manilow fans to contact her via e-mail at acignatti@linkway.com.br. Between her career as a Biomedic and her work in research, she will certainly make time for her Barry Buddies.

*Leslie Millsap and her* mother share a very special bond. Like many mothers and daughters they have many things in common. But in their case, both Leslie and her mother are huge Barry Manilow fans. On several occasions, they have attended Barry's concerts together and one time, they even flew to Boston, Massachusetts, to see him. Their whirlwind excursion originally called for a return flight the very next day. Instead, Leslie and her mother, having never been to the East Coast from their hometown in California, decided to take this rare opportunity to see the sights and take in the spectacular Autumn foliage. Thanks to Barry, Leslie and her mom enjoyed a special "Weekend In New England."

Every Sunday evening, without exception, Leslie and her mother share Barry memories as only a mother and daughter who value the talents of this extraordinary entertainer could. After dinner, they pull out their vast collection of VCR tapes on which they've collected Barry's TV specials and personal appearances throughout the years, and for several hours, they laugh with him, sing along with him and watch his every gesture, smirk, and smile. The event kicks off around 7:30 PM and many times goes as late as 11:00 PM.

How in the world, you may be thinking, are they able to do this without running out of appearances to watch? Simple! After over 20 years in the entertainment industry, Barry Manilow has racked up countless appearances not to mention the many concerts he has given that have been documented and are available for sale. They even possess copies of interviews that Barry has given in England and Japan. The array is endless. "We never, ever get tired of them," Leslie said.

If you are looking for any of Barry's past concerts available on video tape, contact the Barry Manilow International Fan Club or visit Manilow Direct online at www.manilowdirect.com.

As Leslie says, "You'll never run out of good stuff to watch!"

Just a few of the places that have hosted the
"Showman of our Generation"

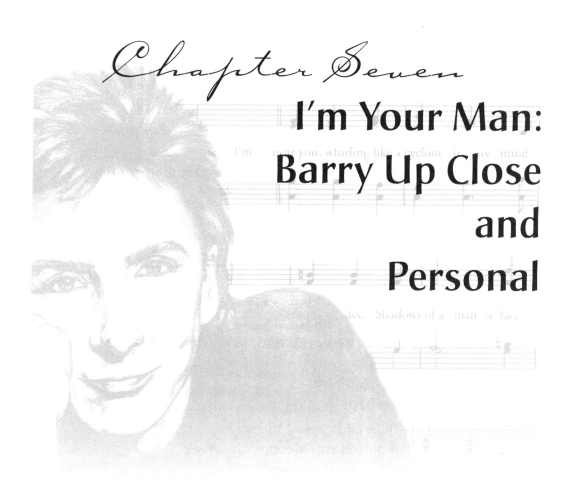

# Chapter Seven

# I'm Your Man: Barry Up Close and Personal

O ver the years, some fortunate fans have had the opportunity to speak to Barry Manilow by phone, meet him personally, or admire him from a distance off-stage. For some who meet him, they have fantasized in detail what they would say to Barry or how their meeting might take place. In their preparation, you would think these fans would have their lines well rehearsed. Sometimes, this is true. Other times, those well thought-out plans fly completely out the window as their lips blurt out phrases that surprise even the people saying them.

The following stories were shared by those fans whose encounters with Barry range from planned surroundings, such as an autograph session, to those completely unexpected.

## We'd Like to Ask Barry....
*Adapted from: 101 Questions We'd Like to Ask Barry*
*provided by:*
*King Of Hearts Barry Manilow Fan Club*

1.  If your house was on fire and you had time to grab one thing, what would it be?
2.  How many copies of your book do you REALLY own?
3.  Does it bother you to know what your fans really think of you?
4.  Would you want any child of yours to follow in your footsteps?
5.  Are you mechanically inclined?
6.  Have you ever awoke in the middle of the night and had no idea where you were?
7.  Do you have any phobias?
8.  Have you ever had to go to the bathroom really bad while on stage?
9.  Do you ever get a bad case of nerves?
10.  Have you ever gotten the hiccups on stage?
11.  Have you ever belched on stage?
12.  What's the strangest thing a fan has ever said to you?
13.  Do you think you'll eventually write another book?
14.  What sort of things do you collect?
15.  Would you go home with me?
16.  What do you eat when you get a sweet craving?
17.  What's the best prank you've ever pulled on your band?
18.  What's the best prank your band ever pulled on you?
19.  What do you do for yourself as a treat?
20.  If you could be someone else, who would you like to be?
21.  What do you do when you can't sleep at night?
22.  How do you approach someone you've always admired and want to meet?
23.  Do you have someone you can really talk to, tell your secret thoughts and feelings to?
24.  Are you happy?
25.  Is there anything your family of fans can do for you?

For some fans, the closest we can get to Barry is by being where he has been. At the walk of fame in Rotterdam, you can feel your hands in his!

*Many Barry fans only* fantasize about speaking to him personally. Ellen Hagarty of Lake Stevens, Washington, was one of those fans whose dream came true. She actually got the opportunity to speak with him by telephone.

While in Washington state, Barry made an appearance at a local TV show, "Northwest Afternoon", where he took phone calls from viewers while on the air. Never knowing exactly what you might get on the other end of the line, one can't be sure anybody could have been prepared for a question like the one Ellen asked.

After telling Barry how much she loves him, Ellen "popped the question." No, not that question. She asked him if he still liked Hamburger Helper. So she was a little nervous.

*It had been a* normal day in the life of Patricia Loram and it looked as if it would end the same. Then, her telephone rang. It was her friend Kathy from Manchester, England, with some good news. Kathy had just learned that Barry would be making a personal appearance in London the very next day, to give autographs. Kathy asked Patricia if she would be interested in accompanying her to the signing. Patricia had to ponder this question approximately 1.5 seconds before she made her decision.

Kathy took the overnight coach from Manchester while Patricia could wait to hop the coach she needed the next morning at 6:00 AM from her home in Bristol. The girls would meet up in London to attend the signing together. Everything for Patricia went as clockwork, until a halting traffic jam just outside of London. Fortunately, this snafu foiled Patricia's plans by making her only 1/2 hour late getting to London. But, the ride wasn't over. Patricia had to hail a cab to transport her to her rendezvous. She flagged down a cab and headed to Oxford Street. She couldn't have asked for better weather. It was warm and sunny outside and in her heart too, for she was off to see Barry Manilow. She arrived at the store where Barry would be appearing, paid the cab fare and ran inside the building. Imagine Patricia's surprise when she rushed in only to discover she was at the wrong store! Patricia left that entrance and hurried up to the other end of the street where she was greeted by a very long "queue." She knew she must be at the right place – finally. She eventually found her friend, Kathy and they made their place in line as they chatted with the people in line around them.

The time arrived for Barry to appear. No Barry. One-half hour later, the store announced that Barry had arrived and he would begin meeting the fans very soon. The line began slowly to move and Patricia started to get nervous, wondering what she would say to Barry, if she could even get

The moment Chistina Cotsifas was picked to be in the CSWY club!

anything out at all. Patricia readied her camera and her CD that she brought for Barry to sign. Her friend Kathy went first and Patricia, like a true "Barry friend," took photos of Kathy getting her autograph. Then, the much anticipated time arrived. Patricia stepped to the table. "I found I was not nervous anymore and as I looked into those beautiful blue eyes, I felt that I was talking to someone I had known for many years, which in fact, was the truth," said Patricia.

Her meeting with Barry lasted only a minute or so, but, she felt as if time stood still. The time had arrived for her to move on and let the next person have their moment with Barry. She wished Barry a safe journey home and moved away from the table. She and Kathy stayed until Barry left then they found a café, had some coffee and recounted the events that had taken place earlier in the day. They eventually made their way back to the coach station to start their individual journeys home. "What a marvelous day," Patricia said "one I shall not forget and can look back on when I feel a little down. Barry Manilow is the best medicine ever invented."

*Before Christina Cotsifas* was chosen as a "Can't Smile" girl, she had another memorable meeting with Barry. In 1989, Christina had an orchid lei flown in from Hawaii especially for Barry. At a concert, she presented it to him and he wore it. Not expecting anything in return, Barry surprised Christina with a kiss that he gave her stage-side.

Is it better to give than to receive? Well, in Christina's case, the receiving was great!

*One of the concerts* Barry performed in 1983 was in Antwerp, Belgium. Unbeknownst to him, Barry "recruited" a brand new fan that evening. This fan joined the BMIFC (Barry Manilow International Fan Club) that very night. The next day, this fan bought every Manilow album available. Only weeks later, this fan traveled to The Netherlands to attend the Dutch Fan Club convention. This new fan was hooked! Longing to connect with other Manilow fans, this new fan placed ads in several local magazines. Along with the very first fan who responded to the ad, they formed Antwerp's first Barry Manilow fan club, "Barry's Friends," only about one year after they met. In 1990, this fan met Barry Manilow. Who is this fan? None other than Passy Schuld, Director of Belgium's Barry Manilow Fan Club.

Passy Schuld backstage at the Apollo Theater in Manchester UK with Barry Manilow.

Passy's meeting with Barry took place immediately following one of Barry's Manchester, England, concerts. After the show, Passy was ushered backstage to a room where food was plentiful and beverages were flowing. Passy was encouraged to help herself to the spread. "Yeah, right," Passy recalled, "as if I wanted to get caught with food in my mouth when Barry walks in!" So, instead of eating, Passy stood in the center of the room with her eyes fixed on the door. The anticipation was almost too much. "I remember thinking what to call him; 'Mr. Manilow' or simply 'Barry.' I didn't want to be rude" Passy explained.

Before long, Passy was being escorted through what to her felt like 50 miles of hallway. Along the way, Passy was greeted by Barry's friendly crew. As photos were taken of Passy and the various what to her felt like-crew members, Barry, tall and handsome, caught Passy's eye as he walked toward her. She was introduced to Barry as the Director of his Belgium Fan Club. "I was very nervous," said Passy, "but Barry managed to calm me down right away. He thanked me for believing in him and supporting him and traveling all this way to come and see him."

Here Passy can't pass up the chance to put her hand in the hand print of the one who has played so much beautiful music for us all.

They talked for a while and throughout the conversation, Barry inquisitively asked Passy questions. "I know I answered the questions but I can't remember any of them," Passy said. "I never thought I'd actually get to meet him in person and when I did, all I could get out of my mouth was that I loved his music and what a great show it had been that night. Talk about silly! If only I could talk to him now…he'd be surprised to what I'd have to say!"

The meeting was a hit and Passy went home to continue her duties as fan club Director with more vigor and enthusiasm as ever. Passy has first-hand knowledge of the entertainer whom she follows and supports so passionately. "He was very friendly and very charming," Passy said about Barry.

♪♩𝄞♪♩

*What is Jennifer Tiner*, a girl from Russellville, Arkansas, doing in a place like Los Angeles? She is making her dreams come true. Jennifer, not by accident, landed a job in television production because of a tip from a friend. Jennifer interviewed for the position and because of her experiences, charm and quick wit, she was the perfect candidate for the position.

But, before her big break, Jennifer worked odd-jobs here and there to make ends meet. Jennifer was once a hostess for a restaurant located in trendy Santa Monica, California. As she was busily taking care of customers one day, she noticed three people enter a quaint shop across the street from the restaurant where she worked. Although the tallest gentleman of the three appeared to be incognito as he made his way through the crowd of people, Jennifer had a feeling somewhere deep in her gut that she recognized the mannerisms of this man. She knew she had seen this man before, somewhere…maybe on a stage?

Jennifer made sure that her station at the restaurant was covered and she dashed across the street to track down this man. Her heart palpitating, Jennifer raced into the store where she saw him enter. Her instincts were right. She did know who this man was. It was Barry Manilow. "I just had to touch him. Somewhere," Jennifer explained. "He was so adorable!" Jennifer mustered up an exuberant, "Hello," and somewhere in their brief encounter, Jennifer mentioned to him that she worked at the restaurant across the street.

Jennifer returned to her job, floored that she had just met Barry Manilow. Her day couldn't have gotten any better, right? Well, it didn't until Barry and the two others he was with showed up at Jennifer's restaurant for a bite of lunch. Jennifer made sure the group was comfortable and being taken care of as she watched the activities of the table out of the corner of her eye.

After the group left, Jennifer was able to rest easy; the pressure was off. Jennifer wanted a souvenir from her famous table, but, being the honest employee that she was, she didn't want to take the fork or glass from the restaurant that Barry had used. Instead, she focused on one, small item that would only be thrown away, to make her very own....the straw from his iced tea.

*Sarah Ingles is a* full-time college student who discovered Barry Manilow and his music in 1994 when she saw him perform "Moonlight Serenade" on the Miss USA Pageant. In Sarah's words, "I was hooked. The song was so beautiful and so was the man singing it." Since that day, Sarah has followed Barry's career; collected his music, attended his concerts and made some great friends along the way.

When Barry came to Sarah's hometown city in Virginia in July, 1997, Sarah wouldn't have missed his performance for the world. Having landed wonderful seats for the show, Sarah anticipated Barry's arrival even more. Unbeknownst to Sarah, a lady whom she met while purchasing her tickets would turn out to be instrumental in what would be the most spectacular experience Sarah has had in her life — meeting Barry Manilow.

Sarah and her friends arrived at the concert and made their way to their seats. In the pre-concert excitement, Sarah soaked up all of the sights and sounds. A relatively new Manilow fan, Sarah has quickly become a veteran of the concert scene. When she was able to meet Barry's manager before the concert, she was honored and thrilled. Little did she know what was in store for her after the show!

The concert was spectacular,but it seemed to come to an end too quickly. When the concert ended, Sarah was approached by the very lady whom she had met when she was purchasing her concert ticket. Sarah was exuberant when she saw her again, but, not as ecstatic as when she discovered what this new friend was going to give to her. Before she knew it, Sarah was holding a backstage pass to meet Barry Manilow. The night couldn't get any better!

Sarah stepped into the line that was forming to go backstage and the lucky guests were ushered into a room where Barry's manager greeted them. Then, the moment of truth had arrived….Barry Manilow walked into the room. He moved from person to person, shaking their hands and exchanging laughs and light conversation. When Barry approached Sarah, she spontaneously asked for a hug from Barry. Her wish was his command. "We hugged and I was melting inside," recalled Sarah. "I told him I was 20 and that this was my 8th show. He asked my name and I told him that my name was Sarah." As Barry and Sarah chatted about the shows she had seen, it suddenly hit her that she was making conversation with Barry Manilow. "I started to cry and shake," said Sarah. "He hugged me again. I told him that I loved him and he said how much that I meant to him. I was in shock!"

Sarah's life was made complete by that one meeting. Sarah eloquently summed up her time with Barry Manilow with these words: "His hands were so soft, he was warm, he smelled so good. He had a lot of make up on still, but, he was beautiful. He was tall, thin, and made me feel at ease. When I asked him if I could hug him, he said 'Sure.' I was so happy, so scared, I didn't know what to do. I saw his eyes and his face, but, most of the time I was in his arms, and there is no other place in the world I'd rather be."

*So far, Gloria Jean Lewis* has met Barry Manilow a total of five times. Her first meeting took place in October of 1987 at a Crown Bookstore in Washington, D.C. She and her "Barry Buddy" Suzanne Swiss made the pilgrimage there from Maryland to have Barry sign their copies of his just released autobiography, *Sweet Life: Adventures On The Way To Paradise*. Gloria and Suzanne wanted to be first in line for Barry's autograph so they arrived at the bookstore the night before his scheduled appearance. Instead of getting a hotel room for the evening and getting up really early the next day to get in line, Gloria and Suzanne did what most hard-core Manilow fans would do to stake their territory in line; they parked directly in front of the bookstore and slept in their car. Actually, they had brought folding lawn chairs and blankets, thinking they would just camp out on the sidewalk all night. But, according to Gloria, they didn't feel extremely comfortable in the neighborhood, all sprawled out on the street, so, the locked car became their makeshift motel.

Sometime during the evening, a couple of people came by to check on Gloria and Suzanne and asked if they needed anything. Gloria gleefully confessed that these angels had been sent by Barry.

Soon it was daybreak. Gloria and Suzanne, feeling much more comfortable due to the dawn, retrieved their lawn chairs and blankets and blissfully prepared their nest, claiming 1st and 2nd in line. Gloria and Suzanne had arrived at 9:00 PM the previous night and it was 12:00 noon when they finally came face to face with Barry.

Every meeting Gloria has had with Barry has been special, but, her third experience was her most exciting time. Gloria had helped out with decorating Barry's dressing room while he was in Concord, California, in July, 1988, and Barry agreed to meet with the fans who put the lavish touches to his dressing room after his concert. During this meeting, Gloria presented Barry with a photograph for him to sign for her. It was an 8 X 10 shot that Gloria's friend Kai Jacques had taken of Barry, which, incidentally, was later used as part of a marquee advertising Barry in concert.

Because of this picture, Gloria, Suzanne Swiss, Christina Young, and Kai were reserved performer tickets for a few of the shows in California. Barry made his backstage appearance, and as he sat down to sign autographs, a line began to form. Gloria and Suzanne hung back to talk with Barry's manager and to thank him for arranging the tickets. Afterwards, Gloria and Suzanne made their way to meet with Barry and Gloria asked him if she could get a picture taken with him. In preparation, Gloria had already instructed two of her girlfriends to be ready with cameras for this special occasion. Barry spontaneously stood up and leaned across the table so Gloria put her arm around his shoulder.

The Mountain View venue performer tickets were beyond Gloria and her pal's expectations. They picked the tickets up at the box office and when Kai opened the envelope, she found four tickets in Row AAA. The gals knew the seats had to be good, but, they had no idea just how good they really were. They referred to the seating chart and there was no Row AAA to be found. However, when the usher escorted the girls to the front of the venue, to their delight there were four padded seats lined up in FRONT of the front row seats. Did their conversation with Barry's manager the night prior have anything to do with their preferred seating? Gloria has no proof for sure, but "we will always feel that it did," stated Gloria.

"I never get tired of seeing Barry perform," said Gloria. "The man puts his heart and soul into every concert he does and there is always something different about each one. I find that when I am watching him perform in person, I am at my happiest. He reaches that certain spot inside me that no one else has ever found. He can make me smile like no one else can. He sings to a crowd of thousands and makes you feel like he is singing to you. There is just some kind of magical connection that happens when he is performing."

*Nancy Matthews and her* friend, Mike had great seats for Barry's performance at The Sands Hotel and Casino in August, 1997. They were seated only about five chairs from the stage at a long table in which the end of the table butted up against the stage. The Copa Room at The Sands has a very private feel, smaller than the majority of stages and arenas where Manilow usually performs. This quaint setting and her fantastic seats afforded Nancy the cherished opportunity to be close to the entertainer she has followed since 1980. More than a decade later, she is still enamored with his voice, grace, and style.

During his electrifying performance, Barry made a move toward the edge of the stage and immediately, the audience members closest to the stage reached out their hands in hopes that Barry would amble over and give them a shake. Seeing what was about to take place, other fans began to approach the stage hoping to get close enough to take the hand of the man who writes and sings the songs. Nancy FROZE! Barry walked to the area of the stage directly in front of Nancy, and Mike noticed that Nancy was not moving toward Barry. Mike didn't want Nancy to miss this once-in-a-lifetime chance to touch Barry. So, what would any true friend do? He pushed Nancy toward the stage.

Barry reached out his hand and Nancy took it. The encounter took only seconds, but Nancy felt as though time stood still. Once Nancy released his hand, she turned around to take her seat. Nancy's face fully described what had just happened. Nancy returned to her seat mumbling over and over, "I touched him, I touched him." Her dream to be close to Barry had come true.

The concert came to an end, and everybody at her table said their good-byes and Nancy and Mike began to exit The Copa Room. But, Nancy wasn't quite finished with her "experience" yet. As they headed for the door, Nancy took it upon herself to share with everyone in her path that she had just touched Barry Manilow. Nancy, who is generally a shy person, approached stranger after stranger. "Excuse me," Nancy said. "I just wanted to let you know that I just touched Barry Manilow." As she walked through the lobby of The Sands, Nancy could be heard telling her tale again and again.

"It was the best thing that has happened to me since the birth of my children," Nancy reminisced. "I'm a pretty boring person but I'm still on a high from that. There is nobody like him. There never will be anybody like him."

*One of Marilyn Meriano's* most favorite "Manilow moments" came in June, 1983. She was attending a Barry Manilow International Fan Club convention at the Schaumburg Marriott in Chicago, Illinois, and one of the convention events was a question and answer session with the one and only, Barry Manilow.

Before the session began, the convention attendees were encouraged to jot down a question on paper and drop it in a box from which Barry would select. As Marilyn approached the box, she noticed the other fans quickly jotting down their questions for Barry. Marilyn's question didn't come that easily. "I stood there, dazed, pondering over what to ask Barry that couldn't have possibly been asked already," Marilyn said. Marilyn had been a fan for at least nine years at that point and although she had never met him, she never felt she would ever feel as closely connected to anyone as she did to Barry Manilow. Marilyn wanted to let Barry know just how much she loved and admired him. Before she could stop herself, pen and paper in hand, she had written the words, "Will you marry me?" and placed the little white piece of paper in the box.

Her friend asked her what she wrote, and Marilyn told her, nervously explaining that Barry would probably not pull her question from the box. After all, he couldn't answer the question anyway, she thought. "It was simply a question that came from my heart," explained Marilyn, "and whether he read it aloud or not didn't really matter."

The large room was set up with chairs and a small stage. Marilyn and her friend sat in the first row to the left of where Barry would be on stage. Barry entered the room, chatted with the audience for a short time, then reached for the box. "In my heart," explained Marilyn, "I hoped that Barry would see my question. Yet another part of me kept saying, 'these questions are usually screened' and my question, by its very nature, would probably be omitted." Marilyn's heart pounded. Would he choose her question? After selecting a few questions, Barry reached into the box and produced another little white piece of paper. "Will you marry me?" were the words that rolled off of his lips. Marilyn sat in shock as her friend screamed, "That's your question!"

There was Barry, the man of Marilyn's dreams, reading the question she so often fantasized about asking him. The complete silence that hushed over both the audience and Barry seemed to go on forever. "I wasn't sure what Barry would do," Marilyn said as she prepared herself for the anticipated and inevitable negative answer. "I kept saying to myself 'no', he's going to say 'no' because he can't say 'yes.' I almost felt sorry, and a little guilty for putting him on the spot like that." When Barry didn't respond right away, Marilyn became concerned about him. "Barry, are you okay?" Marilyn wanted to say to him, "It's okay to say 'no'. I understand." Just then, according to Marilyn, Barry softly said, "yeah," and calmly proceeded with the next question. "At that point," Marilyn recalled, "I thought I had died and gone to Heaven!"

"Barry had made this a special moment for me, one I'll remember all my life. After all, how many times in your life do you have the chance to ask Barry Manilow to marry you and get to hear him answer 'yes,'" Marilyn said. "Even though I know he didn't mean it, it was the nicest thing anyone could've ever said to me."

*Norma Bernsee, her twin* sister, Mimi, and Barry Manilow go back a long, long way. From the moment the sisters heard Barry's music on a PBS Soundstage special, they knew they had stumbled on to something and someone that would change their lives forever.

As teenagers, Norma, Mimi and their friends hit the circuit and traveled to concerts close to their home. They loved the Osmonds, Bobby Sherman, David Cassidy, and of course, Barry. Since none of the gals had their driver's license yet, they had to rely on their fathers to provide the transportation. Norma still remembers how angry her Dad would get as he fought endless traffic after the concerts. But, no matter how angry he appeared to be, he would always take them to their next show.

Although in the late 80's the girls were of driving age, their Dad still drove them to concerts. "My father was the one who was my 'cab driver' to all my concerts since I was 11. I didn't get my driver's license until 1994," explained Norma. Norma lived in the city until a few years ago and there was no need for her to learn how to drive because of the endless availability of buses and cabs. And it was during this time that, after receiving a tip from a reliable source, Norma was informed of Barry's arrival at the airport in the city where she lived. Norma and her sister and a few friends piled into the car, with Dad as their chauffeur once again, and off they went to greet Barry and welcome him to their city. This time, Dad was as excited as the girls.

It was a blistering cold wee hours of the morning as the gals stood waiting for Barry to arrive. Finally, after what seemed like an eternity and frozen toes, Barry's plane arrived. Norma warned everyone to keep their cool. Barry stepped out of the plane and the girls literally froze with emotion. They didn't know what to say until eventually, someone managed a "Hello, Barry."

As Barry stopped to greet his "welcoming committee," he began to sign autographs. When he got to Norma, the pen dropped to the ground as she handed it to him. When Norma bent down to pick it up, she made a highly unusual observation. "He had big feet and nice brown leather shoes," said Norma.

They didn't detain Barry too long as they figured he was tired and it was way too cold to be out. The girls waved to Barry as he walked to his limousine. From the background, Norma's father stepped out and approached Barry, gave him a handshake and thanked him for making the girls so happy.

"Barry became like the family member that came and never left," Norma said. "Even my husband understands and when I first met my husband, I warned him…Barry and my friends are a part of my life and you have to accept this of me. He did and he has."

*Carol Henning remembers hearing* Barry's music in an aerobics class at her local YMCA over twenty years ago. One of their dance routines was choreographed to "Daybreak". Little did she know then that in 1991, she would attend the Barry concert that really awakened her to his charm and charisma and set her on the path to becoming the fan she is today. Carol is the co-director of Manilow Music of Missouri BMFC (Barry Manilow Fan Club) as well as a member of over five other Manilow fan clubs.

One of her favorite Manilow moments happened in June, 1993, while she was at the Las Vegas Desert Inn for one of Barry's performances. After an afternoon of sunbathing, Carol made her way through the lobby to grab an elevator to her room. Looking at the row of elevators, she noticed the door was open to one of them, so she decided to take that one to her floor. She rushed into the elevator without taking an inventory of the passengers. Standing in the elevator were two men with their backs turned to the elevator door. They were in serious conversation as they looked out the glass windows of the elevator. "Then," said Carol, "they turned around and I think my heart stopped." The two men turned out to be Barry and his assistant, Marc. "Barry looked so darn good in his black pants and pink shirt carrying his bottle of Evian," recalled Carol. Menacing thoughts of "should I interrupt them or shouldn't I" raced through Carol's head. Carol decided not to say anything to them and silently took the ride of her life. "It was all too short but, very memorable," said Carol. "I think I still have the bruise marks from kicking myself for not saying something!"

*"We have been on* TV quite a few times. Somehow all TV producers, etc. think it strange that we are so into Barry. They can't believe that as twins we would actually enjoy the same thing," said Monica Jeffress of Bournemouth, England. Monica and her an identical twin sister, Ann Browning, travel the UK and Ireland whenever Barry visits.

What are they doing on TV, you might be asking yourself? On one occasion they were guests on a show in which the studio audience decides who wins a particular debate. In Monica and Ann's case, their dispute was over whether Ann could have an addition built on their house or if Monica should, instead, get to purchase concert tickets to see Barry.

Really, nobody goes away empty-handed from this show. Even though the audience decided that Ann should get her addition, Monica didn't leave broken-hearted. The show host wheeled out a wheelbarrow full of sand to help Ann get started with her project, but buried inside the dirt was a check for Monica's concert tickets. The extension got built and Monica saw Barry.

Probably one of the most unusual television appearances Monica has made was when the BBC in Birmingham dedicated a program entirely to Barry and in tribute to his being there, Monica was asked to decorate a beach hut while live, on air. Monica's old flame and TV personality, Nick Owen arranged for this unique and entertaining charade to transpire. But here's the interesting twist, instead of decorating the beach hut in the usual manner; a few pillows here, a little paint there, Monica was provided specially made wallpaper bearing Barry's face and other sundry items to be placed throughout the beach hut. And if doing this while live on air wasn't nervy enough for Monica, add Barry Manilow watching practically her every move from a monitor in the television studio. The irony of all this was that Monica transformed this beach hut into a cabana in the middle of frosty November.

Nick made sure Monica had a copy of her unusual performance. The next night at the Sheffield concert, Barry's assistant, found Monica and Ann to make certain they had received a video copy of the program. Naturally, they had. They even had made a copy to give to Barry along with some of the wallpaper and photos of the day.

This makeover became a media event as the newspapers also featured Monica in a few featured articles. Monica made sure to clip these accounts from the various papers and added them to her growing scrapbook.

The experience hasn't landed Monica any interior decorating assignments, but, she had a ton of fun putting the touches on the cabana shrine in homage to her favorite entertainer, Barry Manilow.

*When Barry Manilow's musical,* Harmony was playing at the LaJolla Playhouse in LaJolla, California, Nancy Rosebrugh took the opportunity to check it out. She was well aware of Barry's many talents; songwriting, arranging, performing, so she had a pretty good idea that Barry's handiwork in *Harmony* wouldn't disappoint her either.

It was a beautiful, sunny day when Nancy parked her car in the Playhouse's parking lot. Nancy approached the theater and started to take her sunglasses off. As she opened the door, a man exiting the Playhouse was looking down as he put his sunglasses on. Without warning, Nancy and this man literally walked right into each other. As they both excused themselves, the tall, slender man turned to Nancy and asked if she would be seeing *Harmony* that evening. Nancy confirmed that she would be there and the man replied with his hopes that she enjoyed the show and proceeded to the parking lot toward his car.

Nancy froze as her mind began to race and her knees started to shake. Was that who she thought it was? Was that Barry Manilow? Did that encounter really happen? Even though the encounter was brief, she had a very good eye for detail, remembering Barry's royal blue silk dress shirt and his tight, black jeans. And the performance that evening? Spectacular!

*About one month prior* to Barry Manilow's February 14, 1988, concert in St. Louis, Missouri, Mary Vinyard of St. Charles, Missouri, and a bunch of her friends stood in line at the Arena to purchase their tickets. At the same time the girls were standing in line, Jim, a friend, and Mary's mother ran into each other at work and started to talk about Barry's upcoming concert. Mary and Jim often found themselves chatting about her love for Barry's music, so Jim was well aware of how much Barry Manilow meant to Mary. Another friend of Jim's was an announcer at their local radio station, KMOX-AM, so Jim got an idea to call his friend to see if Barry would be visiting the station while he was in town. KMOX-AM was one of the sponsors for the upcoming concert, so it was worth inquiring.

Jim gave his friend a call and sure enough, KMOX-AM was attempting to get Barry to visit their station for an interview. Jim asked what the possibility would be for Mary to meet Barry if he was able to make it. As long as Barry didn't have any objections, neither did the radio station. So, the wheels were set in motion for Mary to meet Barry. The day prior to Barry's arrival, Jim got the confirmation that all systems were "go." Barry would be appearing at the station and Mary, along with her friend Daunna whom flew in for the concert from Utah, would be able to meet Barry.

All of the arrangements were kept secret from Mary until the morning of February 14 when Mary's mom woke her up and told her "You're not going to believe this, but I am 95% sure that you're going to get to meet Barry today." Mary was beside herself. She wanted to know all of the details and how this meeting had been arranged. Immediately, Mary

Mary Vinyard, hanging with Barry.

worried about her friend, Daunna, whom was staying with them. It had been planned for Daunna to meet Barry too, so, Mary was even that much more excited. Mary was told not to call all of her friends as the agreement was that only she and Daunna would be able to meet Barry.

When Mary, her mom, Daunna, Jim, and his wife arrived at the radio station offices, Mary could hardly contain herself. They were brought into a room in which the only thing that separated them from Barry Manilow was a thin glass window. Mary was only feet away from the man of her dreams. Barry had his back to the group as he was being interviewed but eventually turned around and gave them a gorgeous smile. They broke from the interview and the time had arrived. Barry greeted Mary with a big hug. But that's not all Mary wanted. She asked Barry for a kiss and he obliged her and planted a big one right on her lips.

As Mary's surprise meeting came to a close, she told Barry how much his music had changed her life. Mary began to walk out the door but she turned around one last time to see Barry and to say, "I love you, Barry." Barry replied to Mary telling her that he loved her too.

Outside, a group of her friends had gathered to share in this special moment. There were lots of screams, hugs, and tears when they found out that they, too, were going to be meeting Barry later if he could manage to do so. See, Mary also put in that request when she spoke with Barry inside the radio station. And, yes, they too got to meet Barry.

"I will never have a better day in my life, or a better Valentine's Day in my life," said Mary. "I still can't believe everybody knew about it except me, and managed to keep it a secret. I will never forget Jim for this. He made my dream come true!"

*Leslie Millsap of San Mateo*, California, knew the Friday prior to Barry Manilow's Monday night concert in May, 1996 that she would be going backstage after the show to meet Barry. This would be her first encounter with him, face-to-face. There was only a four day span between Friday and Monday, but to Leslie, it felt like at least a month went by before Monday arrived.

Throughout the concert that evening, Leslie was like a cat on a hot-tin roof — nervous, anxious and scared to death. She continually checked her watch as the time ticked closer to the moment she had waited her entire adult life to arrive. The show came to an end, the curtain at the Las Vegas, Mirage Hotel stage fell, lights came up and the theater cleared out. For about fifteen minutes, Leslie and a few others sat in anticipation to make their next move.

A gentleman came to their rescue and escorted the group backstage, and handed them backstage badges. They were now official. They walked into a large room and Barry's assistant, greeted the group and tried to make them all feel at ease. Still wearing the same black, silk shirt that he closed the concert in, Barry appeared; tall and so very handsome.

One at a time, Barry approached each person. "As he walked over to me," Leslie recalled, "he reached out and took hold of my hand. His was soft and warm. He bent down so he could look me right in the eyes. I'm only 5'3" so he had a ways to bend! His eyes are so very blue and so penetrating, almost hypnotic. It's a good thing I remembered my own name!"

Leslie noticed a distinct difference between Barry Manilow, the fabulous entertainer and Barry Manilow, the regular guy. "His voice was so very soft and so low, unlike it is when he's on stage," Leslie said. "In fact, his whole personality changes from being strong and in control to a very sweet, shy, gentle and oh so charming man."

Leslie's car sports personalized license plates, but not the vanity plates that one might expect. Instead of advertising her career or her hobby, her plates pay tribute to her dearest and adored all-around number one man, Barry Manilow. They read "M A N I L O W" with a bright red heart where the "A" would be. And Leslie had brought Barry a photo of her kneeling next to her special plates. On the back of the photo Leslie wrote a short, personal message to Barry and she gave him the photo in which he took and thanked her for.

No meeting like this would be complete without photos to mark the occasion. Leslie and Barry snuggled up close, she putting one hand on the small of his back, the other hand on his belt. "For some reason, God only knows, I put my left hand on his belt buckle," Leslie said. "Believe me, it was totally innocent. I think I just did it so I could balance myself so I wouldn't go tumbling down."

Leslie takes Manilow everywhere she goes.

After the camera went off, Leslie gave Barry a tight embrace. "I didn't ever want to let go," Leslie remembered. Too soon it was time to leave. It was all over and Leslie had survived. "I had a real funny feeling though as I walked back to my hotel room. I wondered, 'Did all that really happen? Was it a dream? Will I ever get that close to him again?' It was almost a lingering sad feeling that made my stomach ache," said Leslie.

Afterwards, Leslie and her friends went out to get a bite to eat. They sat at the table and stared at their plates, speechless. It was as if what they had just encountered hadn't really hit them. Finally, at about 3:30 AM, they started to unwind and celebrate. Their only concern at that point was if their photos were going to turn out okay. They had to wait until noon the next day to find out.

Leslie was pleased with her photo, so much so that she keeps a 5" x 7" of it on her desk at work. Leslie is a receptionist at a law office and many times people, clients and attorneys alike, comment on the beautiful picture. She is constantly being asked if she is either married to or dating Barry Manilow. One lady remarked, "You know, your boyfriend sure looks a lot like Barry Manilow." Leslie went along with the little game for a short time until she cracked up and told her it actually was Barry Manilow. Then the lady remarked, "You mean, you're dating Barry Manilow?" Leslie assures each inquirer that that is not the case, she was simply fortunate enough to meet him and get that wonderful photo.

*What's better than a* 900 number? For Barbara Lovejoy, it was the A&E *Live By Request* telephone line! "You're going to be the first caller" were the words Barbara heard the night of December 5, 1996. They came from the person answering the jammed phone lines at Sony Music Studios in New York City that evening. It wasn't a telethon, by any stretch of the imagination. Instead, Barry Manilow was performing live and taking requests over the phone from the viewers.

The much-anticipated day arrived for the eager and enthusiastic crowd wanting their opportunity to speak with Barry during this special.

Barry would be performing live for two whole hours, so one would think there would be plenty of time to make the call and make your request known. But there were so many questions swimming around in Barbara's head. What songs would he sing? A lot of the old…the new? And by "request," what did that mean? Would someone be cueing Barry on which songs people requested? How would it all work?

The fans were informed that the day of the show, the phone number they'd need to call to make their requests would be posted on the BMIFC hotline. Barbara called and called and called the phone number only to get a busy signal the majority of the day. Finally she got through. She was given the phone number, she wrote it down and then she stared at it. "Barb, there is no way that you are ever going to get through to this number with all the fans that Barry has…there's just no way," Barb told herself.

Ever the optimist, Barbara sat and wrote down all of her favorite Barry Manilow songs and then tried to narrow them down to 20…then 10…then 5. The song that kept popping up on her list was "Weekend In New England." Now, she had the song, her next obstacle: the phone line.

At about 7:45 PM, Barbara dialed the phone number so she could get it on memory to redial. The phone rang twice and then a voice came over the line, "Live By Request." When Barbara finally gathered her senses, she meekly asked, "You're taking requests?" The voice said, "That's why we're here, what song would you like to hear?" She blurted out, "Weekend In New England." The voice replied, "Hold on, I'll see if that is on the list." Barbara was put on hold. She couldn't believe it. She actually got through. Then, Barbara started talking to herself, downplaying the actuality that she would be speaking to Barry Manilow to give him her request. "That song is fine. You'll probably be the third or fourth caller. You might be holding on for over an hour," said the voice. Barbara thought quickly and asked, "Let me ask you something. Will I be talking to Barry?" Yes, indeed, she was assured. "I would hold on all night," Barbara told the operator.

As the time drew nearer for Barbara to be patched through, she and the operator began to make light conversation which included instructions for the caller. The first instruction: don't hang up. Barbara waited an hour and then the operator came back on the line to say, "Barbara, you're going to be the first caller. The next person you talk to will be Barry."

Barbara kept telling herself, "Don't be nervous, it's just Barry Manilow and millions of people listening. You'll be okay."

The VCR was on, the tape was in. It was now 8:59 PM and Barbara heard the music begin. Barry looked gorgeous, shaking hands with the audience.

"It's Barbara from Florida, are you there? Hi Barbara," Barry said. It was then that Barbara realized that she was talking to Barry Manilow on her phone. His voice was coming through her phone! One minute and eight seconds later, Barry started to sing "Weekend In New England" and Barbara hung up the phone and screamed. "This is a memory that I will cherish forever," recalled Barbara. The remainder of the show was fabulous.

"I think A&E did a wonderful job in presenting Barry to the public, generating a renewed interest in Barry and his music and significantly increasing his following, especially among the younger crowd," said Barbara. "I believe this was evident upon the audience which was in attendance during his last tour. The show also allowed people to see what we long-time fans have known for the last 24 years. Thank you Barry for 24 years of wonderful memories."

Barry with Guido Grassi (the director of the Italian Barry Manilow Fan Club)
pose for a quick shot in Atlantic City.
"I was so happy, as to not be able to smile! He was so tired after
a long show . . . "
Still though, in spite of the fact he poured out all of his energy on his audience,
Barry was kind enough to take time for one more picture!

# Chapter Eight

# Barry Manilow Fan Clubs

## BARRY MANILOW INTERNATIONAL FAN CLUBS (BMIFC)

BMIFC*
P.O. Box 45378
Los Angeles, CA 90045
USA
Customer Service: 310-957-5788
Fax: 310-957-5789

BMIFC UK/EUROPE
PO Box 40
Epsom
Surrey
KT19 9EP
England

BMIFC AUSTRALIA
PO Box 138
Randwick, NSW 2031
Australia

BMIFC SOUTH AFRICA
21 Glamorgan Rd.
Parkwood 2139
Johannesburg
South Africa

*The official fan club for Barry Manilow is the BMIFC, located in the United States. All other Barry Manilow Fan Clubs operate within the BMIFC USA guidelines.

# UNITED STATES BARRY MANILOW FAN CLUBS

The following local Barry Manilow fan clubs have been authorized by the Barry Manilow International Fan Club, US (BMIFC). These fan clubs do not offer "official" information about Barry Manilow and his activities. They also do not answer questions or speak on his behalf. They ARE involved in great charity events, gather for club parties and social events, and generally, have fun and make new friends. Contact the club nearest you and get involved!

ON-LINE FAN CLUB

MANILOWS MODEMS
Manimodems@aol.com
www.manilowsmodems.com

*ARIZONA*

BARRYZONA'S SOUTHWEST MAGIC
5735 E. McDowell #3
Mesa, AZ 85215

*CALIFORNIA*

BARRY'S LA LOCALS BMFC
8311 Monique Way
Cypress, CA 90630

A BARRY MANILOW NO FRILLS FC
10 12th Place
Long Beach, CA 90802

PALM SPRINGS HOOTERS
74100 El Cortez Way
Palm Springs, CA 92260

SAN FRANCISCO BAYGELS BMFC
180 Lucinda Lane
Pleasant Hill, CA 94523

NOR CAL IT'S A MIRACLE BMFC
718 Fourth St.
Orlando, CA 95963

SOUTHERN CALIFORNIA BMFC
3718 Mentone Ave. #4
Los Angeles, CA 90034

*COLORADO*

MILE HIGH FOR MANILOW BMFC
9712 Kipling St.
Westminster, CO 80021

*FLORIDA*

BARRY MANILOW RIVER CITY ADM SOCI-
ETY
7268 Old Kings Road South
Jacksonville, FL 32217

*ILLINOIS*

CLUB PARADISE BMFC
153 Michael Lane
New Lenox, IL 60451

HOT TONIGHT FOR BARRY BMFC
PO Box 2954
Country Club Hills, IL 60478

THE IVORY KEYS BMFC
4320 Bloodspoint Rd.
Belvidere, IL 61008

Hot Tonight for Barry Fan Club Members with Di Coleman in Las Vegas

NIGHT SONG BMFC
2917 25th Ave.
Rock Island, IL 61201

WE NEED SLEEP BMFC
342 E. College
Kewanee, IL 61443

CENTRAL ILLINOIS BMFC
122 Oakmoor Drive
East Peoria, IL 61611

IL HOOSIER FRIENDS OF MANILOW
BMFC
1306 Illinois Highway #1, Apt. #18
Carmi, IL 62821

HOPE BMFC
3208 41 Street
Moline, IL 61265

*INDIANA*

RHYTHM OF INDIANA BMFC
PO Box 294
Anderson, IN 46015-0294

*IOWA*

BARRY'S FRIENDS FOREVER BMFC
304 W. State Street
Toledo, IA 52342-1040

Barry Manilow Convention in Memphis, TN 1997
Standing (left to right) — Mary Sells, Marcia Zydorowicy, Ann Kuta, Carol Henning,
Maureen Stojack and Cindee Null.
Sitting —Linda Cox, Friend of Linda, and Judy Martin.

*KANSAS*

ONE VOICE FROM KANSAS BMFC
1430 S.E. 43rd St.
Topeka, KS 66609-1739

*KENTUCKY*

VERY BARRY KENTUCKIANA
CONNECT BMFC
409 N. 28th St.
Louisville, KY 40212-1905

MOONLIGHT SERENADE OF KENTUCKY
326 Valley View Dr.
Radcliff, KY 40160

*LOUSIANNA*

KING OF HEARTS BMFC
130 Northwood Drive
Slidell, LA 70458

*MARYLAND*

MANILOW    MANIACS    OF    MARYLAND
BMFC
11800 Twinlakes Dr. Apt. 611
Beltsville, MD 20705

The L.O.V.E. Barry Manilow Fan Club
Top Row — Betty Sadowski, Nancy D'Agostino
2nd Row — Marge Colorez, Jan Renk, Marlene Babinec, Bobbi Shanahan, Sue Musick
Pool — Ann Underwood, Deb Gajewski, Karen Erickson, Jill Tradel

MASSACHUSETTS

TIME IN NEW ENGLAND BMFC
45 Garden Avenue
Wilmington, MA 01887

*MICHIGAN*

BEAGLE-BAGELS BMFC
25701 W. 12 Mile Rd. #303
Southfield, MI 48034

MANILOW'S MICHIGAN MEDLEY BMFC
190 Ontario Ct.
Lake Orion, MI 48362

*MISSOURI*

MANILOW MUSIC OF MISSOURI BMFC
4045 Weber Rd.
St. Louis, MO 63123

DREAMS COME TRUE BMFC
4502 Cherry Road
Joplin, MO 64804

*NEW JERSEY*

BARRY AND THE MANILOWS BMFC
801 Mulberry St.
Trenton, NJ 08638

The entire group on the Brooklyn Bridge in New York, 1997.

*NEW YORK*

THE FUN BUNCH NYBMFC
60-30 Grove Street
Queens, NY 11385

THE ONES THAT GOT AWAY BMFC
917 Huntington Place
Uniondale, NY 11553

MANILOW MAVENS BMFC
63 Esplande Street
Selkirk, NY 12158

BARRY'S ANYTHING BUT CIVILIANS
BMFC
32 Beechwood Park
Poughkeepsie, NY 12601

BELIEVE IN YOUR DREAMS BMFC
204 Second St.
Syracuse, NY 13209

WESTERN NY MANILOW
MISCELLANEA BMFC
MPO Box 1042
Niagara Falls, NY 14302-1042

*OHIO*

HEART OF OHIO BMFC
535 Pearl Street
Marion, OH 43302

NORTH COAST MANILOW CONNECTION
BMFC
17599 Whitney Rd. Apt. 417
Strongsville, OH 44136

Rhytm of Indianna Fan Club Directors, Carol Trout (left) and Annette Farris.

BUCKEYE CAPITOL CITY BMFC
PO Box 32239
Columbus, OH 43232


*PENNSYLVANIA*

WE GOT THE FEELING BMFC
PO Box 839
North Apollo, PA 15673-0839

PHILADELPHIA BMFC
153 DiMarco Dr.
Philadelphia, PA 19154

IN THE KEY OF B BMFC
600 W. Magnolia Ave.
Aldan, PA 19018

*RHODE ISLAND*

BARRY'S LITTLE RHODIES BMFC
102 Smith Street
Cranston, RI 02905


*SOUTH CAROLINA*

SOMEWHERE IN THE SOUTH BMFC
417 Gwinn Mill Rd.
Pauline, SC 29374


*TENNESSEE*

BEAUTIFUL MUSIC FRIENDS BMFC
3825 Altmira Drive
Chattanooga, TN 37412

"Barry's Friends" attending the BMIFC Europe convention in Eindhover, Netherlands.

*TEXAS*

MANILOW MAGIC BMFC
PO Box 670543
Dallas, TX 75367-0543

BARRY'S ALAMO MANILOWS BMFC
6226 Ingram Road
San Antonio, TX 78238

LONE STAR SERENADE BMFC
1212 Rio Grande
Benbrook, TX 76126

*UTAH*

B-UTAH-FUL MUSIC BMFC
2006 E. Highland View Cir.
Salt Lake City, UT 84109

*WISCONSIN*

L.O.V.E. BMFC
6421 W. Morgan Ave.
Milwaukee, WI 53220

*The data contained herein is subject to change. Please contact the Barry Manilow International Fan Club in California, USA for further fan club information.

# BARRY MANILOW FAN CLUBS OUTSIDE
# OF THE UNITED STATES

*BELGIUM*

BARRY'S FRIENDS BMFC
Eliaertsstraat 1
2140 Antwerp
Belgium

*CANADA*

HOT TONIGHT FOR MANILOW BMFC
19 Fairwood Place W.
Burlington, Ontario L7T 1E4
Canada

*ENGLAND*

MANILOONIES
57 Eltham Park Gardens
Eltham
SE9 1AP
London
England

RAINY CITY CONNECTION BMFC
2 Salisbury Drive
Dukinfield Ches SK16 5DF
England

BIG FUN CLUB BMFC
66 Layton Rd., Parkstone
Poole, Dorset BH12 2BL
England

BARRY'S EXETER FRIENDS BMFC
82 Chard Road
Exeter EX1 3AX
England

BARRY'S ONE VOICE CLUB BMFC
96C Kings Parade Ave.
Clifton Bristol BS8 2QX
England

*GERMANY*

BARRY MANILOW'S GERMAN VOICES
Landgrafenstr.18
10787 Berlin
Germany

*ISRAEL*

BMFC ISRAEL
PO Box 29092
Tel Aviv, 61290
Israel

*ITALY*

BMFC ITALY
285 Via Giustiniano
80126, Naple
Italy

*THE NETHERLANDS*

BARRY'S MUSICAL CLUB BMFC
Niersstraat 18
5626 DW Eindhoven
The Netherlands

*SCOTLAND*

SCOTTISH CONNECTION BMFC
14 Silverknowes Place
Edinburgh EH4 SLS
Scotland

*SWITZERLAND*

BMFC SWITZERLAND
PO Box 897
CH-8953 Dietikon
Switzerland

*The data contained herein is subject to change. Please contact the Barry Manilow International Fan Club in California, USA for further fan club information.

For more fan club information on the net, type www.barrynet.com and click on "his fans".

# A FEW THINGS YOU SHOULD KNOW...

BMIFC HOTLINE
US 626-915-3240
UK 0181-788-4560

STARGLOW DIRECT
Call for Barry Manilow merchandise
Customer Service: 310-957-5788
Fax: 310-957-5789

By mail:
StarGlow Direct
PO Box 45378
Los Angeles, CA 90045

MANILOW ON THE INTERNET
http://www.manilow.com
http://barrynet.com

BARRY MANILOW MUSIC
AND MERCHANDISE
ON THE INTERNET
www.manilowdirect.com

BARRY MANILOW MONTHLY
INTERVIEW LINE
US: 900-737-2672

HELP PHONE
1-310-306-3799

BARRYNETWORK "EXCHANGE"
bmnetwork@aol.com

WANT TO START A
BARRY MANILOW FAN CLUB?
Contact the BMIFC
PO Box 45378
Los Angeles, CA 90045

GO SURFIN!

BarryNet
The Official Barry Manilow Webpage
http://www.barrynet.com

ManiWeb
http://www.netfusion.com/maniweb/index.html

Barry Manilow Superhighway
Bmsh@www.yahoo.com

http://www.netnitco.net/users/grotto/index.html

Barry Manilow's Home Page at Arista Records
http://www.aristarec.com/aristaweb/BarryManilow/index.html

Newsgroup
alt.fan.barry-manilow

* The data contained herein is subject to change. Please contact the Barry Manilow International Fan Club in California, USA for further info.

A drawing by Jeannine Van Eyken-Munch

# Chapter Nine

# A Word from the Fans

"We've grown up with Barry. He was cute and unsure of himself back in the 70s and has grown into a legend in his own time. He will go down in history as one of the greatest musicians of all time. He is our generation's answer to Sinatra. The first teenage fans he had in the 70s are now in our mid 30s…and our children grow up listening to him through us."

*Donna Gosselin, San Antonio, Texas*
*Founder and Director of Barry's Alamo Manilows Barry Manilow Fan*
*Club*

"I have loved Barry Manilow for 18 years. I first heard him on the radio when I was stuck at home with two small children and wondering if my sanity would ever return. I heard 'Even Now' and I felt like I had been punched in the stomach. Someone finally articulated what I was feeling. It was love at first song."

*Gail Lyons, Ontario, Canada*

"I've seen Barry several times (in concert) and when he starts to do the 'Can't Smile' set, I get so nervous that I almost pass out because I cannot sing worth a flip! If I did get chosen as the girl, I'd probably be the first ever to ask him if I could just lip-sync instead."

*Jennifer Tiner, Culver City, California*

"Leave it to Barry to bring his beloved fans into the scene and make us all a part of his fun and entertainment. It was no tryin' to get the feeling again, for our souls were uplifted and exploding with elation long before he threw off his purple jacket to reveal his purple vest, that marvelous mellow voice singing from the heart, 'I'd Really Love To See You Tonight.'"

*Judy Kohnen, Richmond, Virginia*
*Describing her experience at a Barry Manilow concert in 1997.*

"In one word, Barry was masterly. He always creates his own atmosphere with his voice and his lyrics are very profound. He just gave the best of himself, as usual. After all these years, it still gives me the shivers."

*Kathleen Thiry, Antwerp, Belgium*
*Written by Kathleen about Barry's performances in London, England,*
*1998*

"My first Manilow concert was also my first concert ever. I was excited about just being there and seeing Barry in person instead of on my mom's tapes. When he appeared on stage, I saw that he was everything mom said he was. I look back on this day and laugh because I was nine years old and when he appeared on stage I yelled out, 'He's beautiful!'"

*Laura Elizabeth Steed, Slidell, Louisiana*
*13 year old daughter of Robbie Steed and aspiring writer*

"It's just his way with the words, his songs, his personality, the way he moves, the way he laughs which all add up to near perfection."

*Monica Jeffress, Bournemouth, England*

"I've been a fan of Manilow's music for 16 years. His music has given me hope, belief, and a lot of 'kicks in the butt.' What I love about the music and the man is that it is so seldom you see or hear a person who can create music that is one long story. When I play one of his records it is like putting on a book and it never gets boring."

*Pia Sally Jensen, Denmark*

"It is hard to explain what his music does to a person. His music captures you, it overtakes you for the moment. It seems like each song is just for you."

*Patricia Garofola, Bedford, Indiana*

"Just the thrill of Barry when he walks on stage."

*Peggy Gibbs of Plant City, Florida, when asked what her favorite Manilow moment has been in her life.*

"I'll never forget my first concert. I was totally mesmerized. I hung on every single word he said and I could not believe any man could be that handsome and be real! My eyes didn't leave him for a single instant. All I kept thinking was, 'Oh, please, don't let this end!' Of course, it finally did and as he ran off the stage, my heart sank and my stomach ached. I couldn't move. I couldn't get up out of my seat. Then, all I could think about was, 'When can I go and see him again?'"

*Leslie Millsap, San Mateo, California*

"Twenty-four years ago, I fell in love for the first time in my life. It was all the magic you could ever want and at the same time an extreme amount of pain. During the whole experience, Barry kept making beautiful music for us to be in love by. I was so very happy, I thought it would never end. Much to my dismay, it ended so quickly, it ripped out my heart.

Then in late summer 1997, my son gave me tickets to go see Barry. It was the first concert of my whole life, who better than Barry Manilow? I took my daughter and when he sang 'Even Now,' I cried like a baby as my daughter held me.

The good part is Barry makes me realize I am capable of loving someone completely and being without them isn't so bad if you have Barry."

*Susan McCauley*
*Bedford, Indiana*

"We have always been loyal to him. He was never just a 'phase' or a 'fad' which disappeared."

*Susanne Haggberg, Royal Oak, Michigan*
*Speaking about the fans of Barry Manilow*

"If you could bottle a Barry Manilow concert and send it around the world, everyone would be happy."

*Ann Browning, Bournemouth, England*

"I have loved Barry's music for 22 years and always will. Being Such a fan, his music has become a part of me and this is ongoing and not a passing phase. I have had wonderful friendships develop with other fans locally and overseas due to this shared musical passion."

*Louise Jennings, Australia*

"The first time I heard Barry was in a bowling alley. I was going with this guy and he played 'I Write the Songs' on the jukebox and that became 'our song.' I immediately went and bought 'Tryin' To Get The Feeling' and when I turned the album over I saw Barry and Bagel. I thought, 'what a wonderful smile.' Any guy who puts his dog on an album cover can't be all that bad."

*Barbara Lovejoy, Murfreesboro, Tennessee*
*"Can't Smile Without You" girl, December 3, 1997*

"Friendship is what this is all about. Some of my Barry friends are like family. In fact, we are probably closer than family. This never would have happened without Barry."

*Carol Henning, St. Louis, Missouri*
*Co-director Manilow Music of Missouri Barry Manilow Fan Club*

"I always love to see what kind of new things he's going to throw at us (in concert). Everybody always says to me 'Why do you keep going, it's the same thing every time.' I say, 'No it isn't.' Every show is different, some-how. Its just fun getting to see all your friends and traveling to different places."

*Carrie Diener, Beltsville, Maryland*
*(Has seen Barry in concert over 45 times.)*

"My very favorite moment is the moment he comes on stage at every concert that I am at.  It is a privilege to be in the same room as him."

*Christine Smith, West Midlands, England*
*(Has seen Barry in concert over 50 times.)*

"The fans I have met over the years seem to be different and special in that they are very respectful of the place Barry has earned in the music industry.  They have remained completely supportive of his enormous talent despite what the talentless critics have tossed out over the years.  The thing I appreciate most about the other fans is despite the large crowds and obvious affection for Barry, there is literally no pushing, shoving, or obnoxious behavior that prevents others from enjoying the shows.  Thank heavens the fans were smarter than the critics; I think we all knew he would have staying power from the very beginning and we wanted to be along for the journey!"

*Lyn Arnold, Birmingham, Alabama*

"I'd be willing to bet that even the people who criticize Barry have belted out a song or two of his in the car along with the radio!"

*Beth Chase, New Braunfels, Texas*

"In December, 1997, I was able to get my 72 year old mom, Lucille, to fly for the very first time.  She ended up seeing two concerts and having a great time.  I guess the thanks should really go to Barry for bringing out a little bit of the courage we never realized we had, and for filling our lives with the beautiful music he was blessed with and the magical memories of seeing him, that I will cherish and remember forever."

*Marilyn Meriano, Fairfield, Connecticut*
*(Manilow fan since 1974)*

"Barry has originality, sincerity, and honesty plus passion and he's someone to believe in. He makes you feel good."

*Stella Capp, Manchester, England*
*(Has seen Barry in concert over 60 times)*

"Pure and simple, the man's a genius, in writing, singing, arranging, and as a musician. He has done more musically in his career than 10 people normally do in a lifetime."

*Amanda Jo Avery, Fruitport, Michigan*
*Singer/Songwriter*

"He touched my soul with his music—like there was someone out there who really understood me and how I felt."

*Ann Harris, Louisville, Kentucky*
*Officer, Very Barry Kentuckiana Connection Barry Manilow FanClub*

"'Met' is such a vague term! I was never introduced to him. I have never conversed with him. I never sang with him. I've never touched him. I have been within feet of him at several signings. I have looked into his oh so blue eyes. I have spoken with him in those 'just another face in the crowd' instances. And I have loved every one!"

*Betty Sadowski, Milwaukee, Wisconsin*
*President, L.O.V.E. Barry Manilow Fan Club*
*(Answered when asked if she had ever met Barry Manilow)*

"The meaning of 'traveling light' (to a Manilow concert) is not taking all of our Manilow CDs with us."

*Betty Sadowski, Milwaukee, Wisconsin*
*President, L.O.V.E. Barry Manilow Fan Club*

"Barry is the ultimate entertainer, an excellent musician. He is totally devoted to his music; his performances are exciting, vibrant, musically appealing, humorous, and thoroughly entertaining, Barry's talent and charisma radiate when he performs; the countless hours of rehearsal, his demands for perfection, the musicianship that comes from a lifelong devotion to his craft - all of these things are Barry Manilow. I admire Barry's dedication and his constant pursuit of excellence in whatever he does. I admire his intelligence, his energy, his respect for other musicians, his ability to compose, arrange, produce, direct, and perform, and I admire his ability to laugh at himself. And that is why I am, and will always be, a Manilow fan."

*Ann Underwood, Milwaukee, Wisconsin*
*Secretary of L.O.V.E Barry Manilow Fan Club, Milwaukee, WI*
*since 1994*

"I love his voice. It is the most calming and pleasant voice I have heard. As I see him on tour I am also pleased to see that he is funny and giving to his audience and really cares about what his fans want and gives so much of himself in his performance. He seems very down to earth, like a regular guy who is very talented. He is a regular guy, with not a perfect life, but he made it and it gives me hope that pursuing your dreams can work out."

*Carol Tassen, Sterling Heights, Michigan*
*(Working mom of two children)*

"I get sinus infections and my hearing comes and goes. One time my hearing went for three weeks! It was frustrating. I would put one of Barry's tapes in and I'd hear him perfectly! That is why I call him 'my angel of song.' He's a very special man to me. Although I have never met him he touches my soul and heart down to the core."

*Donna Luketic, Cowansville, Pennsylvania*
*(20 year admirer of Barry Manilow)*

"I'm 23 and I've never been to a concert like that (Barry Manilow) before. By the end of the concert, I was totally hooked. It was the best concert I've ever been to; completely entertaining and leaving me wanting more— so much so that the next day I went out and bought 'Summer of '78.'"

*Heather Strouth, New Braunfels, Texas*
*23 year old new Manilow fan*

"The after concert parties were wild! We can't sleep after a show. We need to party in order to prepare for sleep. What a way to live!

*Laura Conners, Rohnert Park, California*
*(talking about the Barry Manilow conventions)*

"I think Manilow (music) will be around for a long time because of his ability to enjoy all types of music and translate them to all ages. He's a very talented individual."

*Martha Fernandes, Riverview, Florida*
*(A Certified Occupational Therapy Assistant and Manilow fan since the early '70's.)*

"His music touches you. It is as if he has looked into your soul"

*Mary Alberstadt, Naples, Florida*
*Barry Manilow fan since 1974*

"His music can stand on its own merit, but the love and support from his fans, I think, has a lot to do with keeping his music alive."

*Mary Boicken, Homewood, Illinois*
*"Can't Smile Without You" girl, December 21, 1997*

"I love his voice. I think he sings from the heart. There is nothing about him that I don't like. I think he is very sincere. I can't even put my finger on it. He is loaded with class. When you go to a show you feel like he wants to be there. He seems very appreciative of the fans. He always thanks the audience and thanks everybody for being with him all these years. I proudly wear my Manilow T-shirts."

*Nancy Matthews, Waretown, New Jersey*

"At my second job, I work in a gift and curio shop at our local shopping mall. During the holidays, I brought in my portable CD player to play Christmas songs while customers shopped. Many of our customers stopped to mention that they liked the particular song that was playing. When I told them it was Barry Manilow, they would say that they really liked him too! Some customers would stay and we would have long conversations of our favorite Manilow concerts, albums, and videos. I really feel that more people are finally finding what we long-term Manilow fans knew from the very beginning. He is one of the BEST!"

*Pamela Jansen, Cape Coral, Florida*
*(Has followed Barry Manilow's career for over 20 years)*

"No kids yet. I'd like twins called Barry and Mandy!"

*Passy Schuld, Antwerp, Belgium*
*(replied when asked if she had children)*

"His music just makes you feel. It makes you think and reflect. It touches your soul. What has kept me a fan all these years is also all the different avenues Barry has taken with his music, from *Showstoppers* to *Broadway* and *Swing Street*. His talent is endless and for me that is what keeps me coming back with quiet anticipation asking…what will you delight us with next Mr. Manilow?"

*Sabrina Lowd, Decatur, Georgia*

"At work, when I put in for vacation time, I get asked, 'Where is Barry playing now?'"

*Sandy Lapiska, Orlando, Florida*
*"Can't Smile Without You" girl, November 19, 1995*

"Most of us have followed Barry for many years and supported everything he has done. His music and personality has inspired a lot of us and affected our lives. Similarly we believe that Barry's life has been affected by having us around all these years and so there is a mutual bond between us all that goes way beyond just the music."

*Susan Love*
*Barry's One Voice Barry Manilow Fan Club, Bristol, England*

Dear Mandy,

We met at the Copacabana and spent the Weekend in New England. Even Now, I Don't Want to Walk Without You. So, This One is For You. I Am Ready to Take a Chance Again. You are probably saying to yourself that It's a Miracle but, I ask myself, Could it be Magic? Who Knows? I just know I Can't Smile Without You. I would sail 50 Ships to reach you by Daybreak. Let's Hang On. Somewhere Down the Road, The Old Songs will make us feel Lonely Together.

Looks Like We Made It!

Signed,

Some Kind of Friend

Written by Lynne Holland, Marketing/Publicity
Frank Erwin Center, Austin, Texas

# For You. . .

by: Debbie Waldron
Virginia Beach, Virginia

$\mathcal{S}$o it starts

The piano singing out the first chord—first flutter of a melody

Asy your heart takes flight in a whirlwind of anticipation

The song beckoning you on, calling with each strum of a note.

Tones whisper a simple sweet song for you

Singing out dreams, hopes and desires

Fantasy sounding out with each lyric gently murmured

You quietly singing along to the tune—faintly

The lost promise of love spoken in its woven spell

Touching upon your hearaches.

And the music grows into an echo, as the mist fills your eyes—words

of the song so very hard to remember

You hold your hands tight in comfort,

closing your eyes as the last note plays out

So Dream like

Like a lone butterfly dancing in the wind.

Once over, the spell is broken, the lights are brightened, as you stand

to leave—wondering where the time went

Wondering when you can come back

Lost hopelessly, wondrously, all in just a few hours.

Humming as you leave

Smiling as you go

Knowing all the time the music, the glances,

the special moves, were all meant for you

For you. . . the fan.

# The Musician and the Writer

by: Linda Horner
East Sussex, England

The musician and the writer
Come together and make a song
They write about their feelings
About life and when love goes wrong.
The music has the power
The words go hand in hand
The musician and the writer
Both feel and understand.
The passion lies within them
It has to be let out
That's what words and music's for
They know what it's all about.
If you take away the music and take away the words
Then you take away the harmony
With no song left to be heard
The words are there inside your head
They are written from the heart
All this time I knew they were mine
The words that had to be said.
A musician has the music
A writer has all the words
Together they go in harmony
A song that needs to be heard.
As we listen to the melody
We take in all the words
A melody that sounds so sweet
And words we can relate
Where would we be without a tune?
Days gone by without the silvery moon
Where would we be without the words
Not to be written, not to be heard.
For me they make the perfect sound
A perfect match is what I've found
They go together hand in hand
So we can feel and understand.
The passion lies within them
It has to be let out
That's what words and music's for
That is what it's all about.

*Dedicated to Barry Manilow and Bruce Sussman*